D1122021

Form, Meaning, and Focus
in American Sign Language

Kristin Jean Mulrooney, General Editor

Form, Meaning, and Focus in American Sign Language

Miako N. P. Rankin

GALLAUDET UNIVERSITY PRESS

Washington, DC

Sociolinguistics in Deaf Communities

A Series Edited by Kristin Jean Mulrooney

Gallaudet University Press

Washington, DC 20002

http://gupress.gallaudet.edu

Library of Congress Cataloging-in-Publication Data

ISBN 1-56368-573-6; 978-1-56368-573-6

ISSN 1080-5494

⊚ The paper used in this publication meets the minimum requirements of
American National Standard for Information Sciences–Permanence of Paper
for Printed Library Materials, ANSI Z39.48-1984.

Contents

Editorial Advisory Board

Acknowledgments

I would not have been able to write this book, or the dissertation on which it is based, without the support of my dissertation committee members. Thank you, Paul Dudis, for being my advisor. The hours we have spent discussing these fascinating issues, considering patterns in the data, and making cross-linguistic comparisons are the true embodiment of the academic endeavor, and I cherish those moments. Your insights were, and are, invaluable. You continually challenge me, digging deeper, and always asking the next question (and the next one, and the one after that, too)—and for that I am deeply grateful. I have grown intellectually through this process, and it is thanks to you. Deb Chen-Pichler and Kristin Mulrooney, thank you for the time and energy you devoted to my success, always believing in the potential of my work and presenting a clear road map to get me there. My sincere appreciation also goes out to both Cynthia Neese-Bailes and Michel Achard for your wisdom, expertise, patience, and feedback all along the way.

I would not have made it to this point in my academic career without the support of the faculty of the Department of Linguistics. You all gave me the tools to succeed, the foundational knowledge to explore this field, and continuing guidance throughout the process. As my professors, my mentors, my colleagues, and my friends, you were always there for me, and I thank you.

I would not be in this field without the support of the Deaf community. All along my journey there have been guides and friends and role models. It would be impossible to name you all, but do know that I hold you close to my heart and I am beholden to you. Most importantly, I must thank those who first welcomed me into the Deaf world and shared their language and culture with me: the staff and students of the Colorado School for the Deaf and the Blind. Jeanette Scheppach, Pammie Wilding, Barb Kerek, Tim Elstad, Ralph Arellano . . . the list goes on—this book, like everything else I do with potential positive implications for the Deaf community, is because of you. You impacted my life in incredible ways, and the ripples of your impact reach far and wide.

I would not be here at all without the support of my family and friends. Again, too many to name, and all so important. Thanks to you all for sharing your lives with me, giving me the energy to keep going, and reminding me of the importance of balance. Mama, Papa, Kaselel, Jason—your love sustained me though this book, and I know that its sustenance will continue through whatever comes next. Thank you.

Editor's Note

Ceil Lucas wrote that her goal for the Sociolinguistics in Deaf Communities series was to "provide reports of current research on all aspects of sociolinguistics in Deaf communities, bilingualism and language contact, variation, discourse analysis, language policy and planning, language attitudes" (Lucas 2010, xv). In this volume, Miako Rankin elegantly guides us thorough the careful examination of how American Sign Language (ASL) expresses nonagent focus. She highlights for us the purpose of language—to convey meaning—and asks us to use that as our starting point for linguistic inquiry. Of interest here, if a person is using ASL, and does not want to explicitly mention the agent of the sentence, how is this accomplished?

Does this fascinating description of the linguistic constructions available in ASL connect to this series? Dr. Rankin answers this in the first sentence of the book: "Teeming with thoughts, the human mind by nature desires to connect with other human beings." This is why language exists—to connect and socialize with others. The deeper our understanding of the linguistic structures, the closer we are to explaining how we connect. Returning to nonagent focus, there are times when we do not wish to disclose who is involved in an action. The reasons are many and often involve social motivations. Dr. Rankin continues the discussion of how this is accomplished in ASL. In so doing, she provides the foundation for this information to be examined in different discourse settings, how it varies across users, how it can be taught to second language users . . . you see how this fulfills Dr. Lucas's vision.

I hope you enjoy reading this book as much as I did seeing it develop. I anticipate you will feel the energy Dr. Rankin brings not only to this topic, but also her passion for sharing these ideas.

Kristin J. Mulrooney
Washington, DC
September 2013

REFERENCE

Lucas, C. 2010. Editor's Note to *Language Policy and Planning for Sign Languages*, by T. Reagan, xv. Sociolinguistics in Deaf Communities 16. Washington, DC: Gallaudet University Press.

Form, Meaning, and Focus
in American Sign Language

Chapter 1

Introduction

Teeming with thoughts, the human mind by nature desires to connect with other human beings. Our thoughts are dynamic and multifaceted. They range from the mundane to the extraordinary, and from moment to moment we seek to communicate statements of the directly and presently tangible as well as flights of fancy and intricate abstractions. We recognize that other humans are experiencing such complexity of thought as well, and to live in community we need and want to share our thoughts with them and be privy to some of their thoughts as well. For everything from planning to politics to poetry, the primary means by which we attempt this feat is language.

Language use is not direct access to thought, however. In communicating even what seem to be simple concepts, we make choices about how much detail to express, which perspective to convey, what aspects to emphasize. On all of these scales, languages allow for various choices while limiting others. At the lexical level, we may choose to describe the same person using the words *that boy* or *the young man in the yellow T-shirt* or *David* or *your annoying brother.* This multiplicity of options applies not only at the lexical level; it is also available to us as we combine words into utterances, and we can describe a single event in various ways.

The English sentences in examples 1 through 3, for instance, could be uttered as descriptions of the same event, yet each one expresses a different portrayal of that singular event:

1. Scott bought the painting from my sister.
2. My sister sold the painting to Scott.
3. The painting was sold to Scott (by my sister).

The primary distinction conveyed here is what cognitive linguists refer to as *construal,* which is defined as the specific portrayal of a given situation (Van Hoek 1997; Langacker 2001; Taylor 2002). Although all three sentences describe the same event and they can all be simultaneously accurate representations of what occurred, they do not all convey the same meaning. Each sentence asks the reader to conceptualize the situation differently. In sentence 1 the focus is on Scott and his action; in sentence 2 the sister is the most active participant; and in sentence 3 the painting itself is the primary focus. Though all three express descriptions of the same event and resultant state, different circumstances would call for each one, depending on which aspect of the scene the speaker chooses to emphasize. A native English user would not use them interchangeably. Construal is therefore a critical component of meaning.

THE MEANING OF GRAMMAR

The sentences in examples 1 through 3 express different construals through both word choice and grammatical structure. Sentences 1 and 2 both have the same grammatical structure. The difference between them is the choice of the verb, namely, *bought* in sentence 1 and *sold* in sentence 2. Sentence 3, however, uses the same verb as sentence 2 (i.e., *sold*), but its grammatical structure is different from that of sentences 1 and 2. This difference allows the same situation to be expressed by yet another construal.

Sentence 3 is in passive voice, whereas sentences 1 and 2 are in active voice. In active-voice utterances, the participant initiating the action, called the *agent,* is expressed in subject position and is understood to be the focus of the utterance. In a passive-voice utterance, the agent is not the focus of the sentence; the agent either is not expressed at all or is expressed in a *by*-phrase that occurs after the verb. This structure evokes a meaning in which the agent is not in focus.

Since various construals can be expressed by choosing different lexical items, such as the verbs in 1 and 2, or by choosing particular grammatical structures, as in 2 and 3, grammatical structures themselves convey part of the meaning of expressions. In fact, as Langacker (2006) states, "The semantic import of grammar resides in particular ways of construing the conceptual content evoked by other elements" (115). The meaning of each sentence depends not only on the meaning of the individual words but also on the meaning provided by the construal, which is based on the grammatical arrangement of those words.

For language learners, the fact that particular forms evoke particular meanings at all levels—morphemes, lexical items, grammatical constructions, discourse structures—has striking implications. In addition to understanding the vocabulary of a new language, an effective language user must also be able to recognize patterns in the use of particular grammatical constructions in order to be able to generalize over a variety of situations and determine the meaning encoded in the various forms of the sentences. This understanding of structural meaning is the foundation of one's expressive ability and allows one to form novel sentences and converse comfortably in a range of discourse settings.

Fortunately, the importance of learning vocabulary in context and of being able to use the appropriate constructions is generally understood. We know that replacing English words with "equivalent" Spanish words does not yield an effective translation, as evidenced by the hilarity (or downright weirdness) that can ensue when performing such "word-to-word translations" via web-based searches such as Google Translate. It goes without saying that students of a language who learn vocabulary but have no clear understanding of the ways in which constructions at the phrasal, sentential, and discourse levels interact with that vocabulary will be ineffective at conveying their true intent.

Unfortunately, this seemingly commonsense understanding that meaning in language stems from so much more than vocabulary alone is somehow less self-evident when the languages under consideration are a spoken language and a signed language. Formal linguistic analysis of signed languages is a relatively recent undertaking (generally considered as getting its real start with the work of William Stokoe in the early 1960s; Stokoe 1960; Stokoe, Casterline, and Croneberg 1965) and as such the extent of what we know about grammatical and discourse structures remains quite limited. Though our foundation is strong and the field is blossoming as it reaches the half-century mark, linguistic knowledge about American Sign Language (ASL) as used by those who acquire it natively from their parents has not been able to keep pace with the demand for teaching ASL to aspiring students. This, in combination with myriad sociological and biological facts about deaf lives and signed languages (Padden and Humphries 1988; Van Cleve and Crouch 1989; Lane, Hoffmeister, and Bahan 1996; Padden and Humphries 2005), conspires to create a situation in which vocabulary teaching takes precedence. As a result, a true grasp of the meaning conveyed at other levels is often missed.

PASSIVE VOICE AS A CASE STUDY

Take passive voice as just one example. Many materials designed for teaching ASL and/or for teaching ASL/English interpretation and transliteration (Kelly 2001; Mikos, Smith, and Lentz 2001) maintain that ASL does not have passive voice and that agents must therefore be in focus. Students are taught that agents should always be overtly specified in prominent positions (i.e., at the beginning of an utterance and expressed as either a topic or the subject), and interpreters are encouraged to produce "active" signed translations of spoken utterances expressed in passive voice.

If beginning users of ASL are going to be interpreting, there is good reason for teaching them to restructure English passives into active ASL structures. Literal translations of passive utterances in English generally leave out the morphemes that mark verbs as passive (a form of *to be* and the past participle of the main verb), resulting in an expression that literally reverses the roles of agent and patient.

Consider, for example, this short text about an experiment on REM sleep:

REM Sleep Experiment

Experiments show that REM sleep definitely can help you learn better. In one test, volunteers were taught a new skill. That night, some of them were awakened whenever they entered REM sleep. The others were awakened the same number of times, but only during non-REM sleep. The next day, the people who got their REM sleep tested better than the others at performing the new skill.

The main clause of the second sentence is "volunteers were taught." A literal translation that followed the English word order and omitted the passive markers would potentially be VOLUNTEERS TEACH, incorrectly stating that the volunteers were the ones doing the teaching rather than the ones learning the new skill.

The following sentence in the English text ("some of them were awakened") is also in passive voice, and a literal translation omitting the passive marking would again result in a skewed meaning, though in this case the effect on the meaning is quite different. Here an attempt at translation that ignores the content conveyed by the passive structure would result in the ASL utterance SOME PRO.pl→volunteers WAKE-UP. Because the volunteers are expressed as the subject of the active verb WAKE-UP, the meaning conveyed is that the volunteers woke up of their own accord, which is not the meaning conveyed in the original English sentence and in fact skews the entire understanding of the experiment.

Thus, teaching beginning students of ASL, who are producing word-by-word literal translations of the English sentences in their heads, to recognize agents and express them actively in ASL makes sense. However, the underlying assumption that in ASL agents must always be in focus is untrue.

If it were true that agents must always be in focus in ASL, one would expect ASL users, when asked to translate English passive sentences into ASL, to produce only utterances with an agent-focused construal. They might express all assumed agents overtly as subjects. For English prompt sentences with *by*-phrases, one would predict that ASL users would reorder the entities to produce an utterance with the agent in subject position.

However, in data collected for my dissertation, when native ASL users were asked to do precisely that—translate English passive sentences into ASL—only 11 percent of the utterances they produced had the agent in focus. Within the set of twenty sentences containing passive-voice clauses, three of the passive prompt sentences even included overt mention of the agent (i.e., in a *by*-phrase). Even from these prompts, where rearrangement to produce an ASL utterance with the agent in subject position is remarkably straightforward and would be expected, participants reordered the entities only half of the time. Even more striking, out of eighty given opportunities, signers chose to overtly express an assumed agent in only four instances.

Clearly, ASL users do have ways to express a construal in which the agent is not the primary focus. The goal of my dissertation research and this book describing those results was to determine the linguistic strategies that ASL users employed to express a meaning similar to that expressed when English speakers use passive voice. The data showed that, in ASL, just as in English and other languages, various linguistic factors influence the level of focus with which entities are construed. In addition, ASL has multiple mechanisms for achieving agent impersonalization, and each mechanism, with its unique form, results in a slightly different construal.

The motivation for undertaking research on passive voice specifically began with my experience teaching English reading and writing to deaf students. Although the students were working hard to understand the material, I found myself struggling to explain the meaning expressed through particular English grammatical structures. In our classroom, ASL was the language of instruction, so part of my role in explaining the structures included providing ASL translations of the English example sentences. For passive voice in particular, I found myself unable to come up with ASL expressions that were semantically equivalent without resorting to long, drawn-out explanations and roundabout explanations of meaning. I wondered how native ASL users express the meaning encoded in passive utterances, specifically the reduction in focus on the agent in a transitive event. What started as a query related to improving my effectiveness in the classroom naturally evolved into my research question and the design, elicitation, analysis, and results described in this dissertation.

Using my classroom experience and understanding of the meaning of the English passive as a foundation, the research question I formulated was therefore as follows: does ASL have structures that evoke a defocused agent construal? The requisite follow-up question was of course this: if so, what are the forms of these ASL agent-defocusing utterances? Once utterance types that defocus the agent had been identified, further analysis was conducted with the goal of describing how the utterances shift focus away from the agent and what level of agent focus each utterance type evokes.

Because the motivation for the research emerged from my personal teaching experience, in which I had struggled to find equivalent translations for passive sentences, similar translation tasks were used to elicit the data. Four participants, all native ASL users with advanced proficiency in written English, were asked to translate individual English passive sentences and short written English texts containing passive constructions into ASL. They were also asked to do a short ASL-to-English translation task for comparison.

Though using translation for elicitation purposes has potential drawbacks, I chose it as the starting point for this initial foray into the question of how ASL expresses defocused agent construals. The use of passive prompts in English controlled for the target defocused agent construal, so the task required the participants to either produce ASL utterances that evoked the same construal or restructure their utterances in a way that would express analogous meaning. Because the tasks involved translation, specific participants who are skilled bilinguals with advanced metalinguistic awareness were chosen, thereby reducing the potential negative impact of working with both languages during the elicitation tasks.

The elicitation tasks were designed to investigate several different aspects of ASL expressions evoking defocused agent construals. Isolated passive sentences in English were used as prompts for one task in order to determine how ASL users express events when the agent is entirely unknown. I was curious to see what structure(s) would be employed and whether patterns would emerge. In the other task, the short texts containing English passives were each representative of a different discourse genre and were included to determine whether pragmatic similarities exist between ASL and English (i.e., whether similar construals would be evoked in the ASL texts or whether the signers would simply restructure the content as a whole and produce agent-focused utterances).

In fact, in the collected data, the most common strategy that native signers used to produce translations of English passive sentences was to simply leave the agent unexpressed. Though claims have been made that ASL is more direct than English (see discussion in Hoza 2007) and that ASL uses active voice where English uses passive voice (e.g., Kelly 2001), native ASL signers who were asked to translate English passive sentences into ASL simply added overt subjects and changed them into "active" sentences in very few cases. Participants did not struggle with the translation tasks they were given, and they expressed very little discomfort at being asked to produce agent-defocused construals. All four signers in all of the translation tasks readily produced utterances that simply did not overtly mention the agent, evoking the defocused agent construal.

In addition to the fact that agents were not always overtly specified, various levels of agent focus were also found to be expressed in ASL, just as in English and other spoken languages. These ASL utterances encode construals that parallel those encoded in the range of impersonal forms in English, in which prominence and specificity interact to produce various degrees of agent focus. Just as English uses not just the passive voice but a variety of other impersonal forms as well, each of which defocuses the agent to a different extent (Shibatani 1985; Marín-Arrese 2008), ASL also has a variety of impersonalization strategies that reflect different ways agents can be expressed and also affect the degree of focus on the agent.

Based primarily on my dissertation research, this book explores the options for expressing agents in ASL. Such information on where and how agentive entities are expressed, as well as the varying levels of focus evoked by each form, expands our knowledge of the intricacies of meaning inherent in particular ASL constructions. Perhaps more important, though, this book also demonstrates that form can never be divorced from meaning at any level, reminding us that for true understanding we must look beyond vocabulary.

Chapter 2

Foundational Concepts

The primary content of this book is the description of the various levels of focus with which agents of events can be expressed in American Sign Language (ASL). Before we get to the details of the ASL data, however, we need to look more closely at the direct link between meaning and form. Let us thus consider the range of impersonalization strategies that occur in English and use them as a foundation for the analysis of the ASL data in the following chapters.

Because we are honing in on a particular aspect of *meaning* and describing the syntactic *forms* that native ASL signers use to evoke that meaning, cognitive linguistics, which focuses on the relationships between meaning and form, serves as the theoretical framework guiding the analysis. Within this framework, I use diagrams and terminology based on Ronald Langacker's theoretical model of Cognitive Grammar (CG) to describe the constructions in the elicited data. The result is a cognitive linguistic–based overview of the resources available for describing events with the agent evoked at various levels of focus.

FOUNDATIONAL CONCEPTS FOR UNDERSTANDING LANGUAGE

Language is a systematic means of symbolizing conceptualizations through phonological forms. The linguistic resources available for describing events are highly motivated by our human experience of events themselves:

[C]ertain recurrent and sharply differentiated aspects of our experience emerge as archetypes, which we normally use to structure our conceptions insofar as possible. Since language is a means by which we describe our experience, it is natural that such archetypes should be seized upon as the prototypical values of basic linguistic constructs. (Langacker 1991, 294–95)

The clause structures that exist in languages are primarily grounded in these archetypal experiences. For example, prototypical active sentences convey an event in which an agent acts upon a patient, creating some kind of change. The active sentence structure reflects events we have seen over and over again in our lives. Events evoked in active sentences therefore are coded in a structure parallel to "the canonical way of apprehending what is arguably the most typical kind of occurrence" (Langacker 2008, 357).

In cognitive linguistics, expressions are understood to structure their semantic components in particular ways (Talmy 2003; Langacker 2008; Verhagen 2007). Cognitive Grammar (Langacker 1987, 1991, 2008) posits that only three types of structures are necessary to achieve this semiological function: phonological structures (the form of the morphemes, words, phrases, sentences, discourse, and so on used in the language); semantic structures (the meanings associated with those forms, which includes denotation and connotation, as well as the discourse functions, of those forms); and the symbolic links between phonological structures and semantic structures.

Within this framework, lexical items and grammatical structures, as well as items at all other levels of linguistic expression, are understood to be conventionalized symbolic structures in which form and meaning are inextricably linked. In this view the conventional units that language users control in the inventory of a given language include not just morphemes and lexical items but also the schemas for the grammatical patterns of that language.

All linguistic expressions instantiate schematic patterns. For example, in the utterance "Sally made dinner," the words *Sally* and *dinner* are instances of the noun schema, the word *made* is an instance of the verb schema, and the entire phrase is an instance of the schema for noun-verb-noun clause structures. As we use words and phrases, our minds process the individual expressions and abstract away from specific instances to also recognize schematic relationships between the current expression and others we have seen or heard.

Cognitive linguists consider language capability to be usage based (Tomasello 2003; Lieven and Tomasello 2008). Each time an expression is used, the schema it instantiates is activated. Over the course of multiple activations, the schematic similarities between multiple uses become increasingly entrenched, allowing the schema to be used more readily in the comprehension and production of novel expressions. "The semantics of the clausal patterns [are] based on fundamental patterns of experience, acquired through a process of categorizing over learned instances" (Goldberg 1998, 215). In other words, the more often one has heard, seen, and used a particular type of expression, the more comfortable one will be with its use.

Linguistic units consisting of a form and meaning correspondence, including grammar-construal correspondences like active voice and passive voice, are referred to as *constructions* (Goldberg 1995). In addition to learning the conventional ways to use words (which requires knowing the forms and understanding what they mean), language users also learn the conventional ways to use grammatical constructions. Although language users do not need to be able to make their metalinguistic awareness explicit in order to be effective at using a language, they must be able to recognize the schematic form of grammatical structures and understand their inherent meaning.

To summarize, any schematic construction such as the English passive "captures a general pattern for the combination of smaller units into a larger assembly" (Taylor 2002, 589). The conceptual content that constructions invoke consists of symbolic structures, which are links between semantic and phonological structures (Langacker 2000). A certain combination of symbolic structures evokes a particular construal, which is then understood as the "meaning" (conventionalized usage) of that construction.

DISCOURSE FUNCTION OF PASSIVE VOICE

Utterances impose a particular construal on the event they express. In other words, the syntactic form of an utterance provides information about how the concepts within that utterance are to be structured. In English, active voice or passive voice may be used to describe an event in which one participant acts on another. In an active-voice utterance, the participant initiating the action, called the *agent,* is expressed in subject position and is understood to be the focus of the utterance. The basic form of the English passive (i.e., patient expressed in subject position, a form of *to be,* and the past participle of a transitive verb) evokes a construal in which the agent is defocused. Including a *by*-phrase can add a slight focus to the agent, but because of its less prominent position, it will remain reduced in focus relative to the agent in an active utterance.

Thus, the difference between utterances in active voice and passive voice is a difference of construal.

Across instances of passive sentences, the defocused agent construal is always evoked. Defocusing the agent is the key component in the meaning of the passive voice (Shibatani 1985), as reflected in the pragmatic reasons that passive constructions are used (identified by Jespersen 1924, in Shibatani 1985):

- The active subject is unknown or cannot easily be stated.
- The active subject is self-evident from the context.
- There may be a special reason (tact or delicacy or sentiment) for not mentioning the active subject.
- Even if the active subject is indicated ("controverted subject"), the passive turn is preferred if one naturally takes a greater interest in the passive than in the active subject.
- The passive turn may facilitate the connection of one sentence with another. (Shibatani 1985, 830)

In all of these pragmatic uses of the passive construction, the most important component of the construal is that of reduced focus on the agent. The fact that English passives evoke defocused agent construals of events led me to consider more deeply what ASL constructions might evoke a similar construal and therefore serve these same types of pragmatic function.

Different languages may use different construction types to evoke similar construals (Talmy 2000). Passive constructions serve to defocus the agent, but they are not the only way to achieve this purpose. In seeking to understand how ASL evokes a construal similar to that of English passive constructions, my goal was not to determine whether ASL has passive constructions or what the structure of a passive construction in ASL would be if one existed (for such analyses see Wilbur 1987; Isenhath 1990; Kegl 1990; Janzen, O'Dea, and Shaffer 2001) but rather to determine what ASL structures can be used to evoke defocused agent construals regardless of whether they are expressed as passive or some other type of construction.

UNDERSTANDING FOCUS

Before we consider constructions that evoke reduced agent focus, we need to understand the factors that create salience within linguistic entities. To do so, let us take a closer look at the example sentences from chapter 1:

1. Scott bought the painting from my sister.
2. My sister sold the painting to Scott.
3. The painting was sold to Scott (by my sister).

Semantically, the verbs *bought* and *sold* are both *multivalent verbs,* which means that they encode a relation and its two (or more) participants. The relation they encode is one in which an item changes hands in exchange for money. *Bought* and *sold* both also encode three entities: an item that is changing hands; the "seller" (i.e., the person who originally owned the item that is changing hands); and the "buyer," who will end up owning the item. In this situation, described in sentences 1 through 3, specifically, the "item" is the painting, the "seller" is my sister, and the "buyer" is Scott.

In these sentences, one major difference in construal is the relative prominence of the entities involved. This difference comes from the profile structure inherent in the meaning of each verb. The verb *bought* in sentence 1 sets up an asymmetry of prominence that places the focus on the buyer, while the verb *sold* in sentence 2 establishes an asymmetry that focuses on the seller. The passive-voice construction in sentence 3 evokes a prominence asymmetry that focuses on the item itself.

Prominence asymmetries are evoked by the profiling of a certain aspect of a conception against a broader conceptual background (Langacker 1987; Taylor 2002). Linguistic expressions designate their conceptual referent by virtue of this profiling. To take a simple example, the word *knuckle* profiles a particular portion of a finger. The conceptualization of a finger is necessary as the base against which the concept of a knuckle may be understood. At a broader level, the word *knuckle* also invokes more general information, such as the conceptualizations of a hand, an arm, a body, and so on. This broad knowledge, which serves as background for both the particular profiled element and its base, is known as the *domain.* Thus the use of the word *knuckle* is understood to profile the joint of a finger (its base) within the domain of a hand/arm/body.

The notion of profiling is essential for CG definitions of grammatical categories like noun and verb, which are based on what they profile (Langacker 1987). Nouns, by definition, profile things, while prepositions, adjectives, and verbs profile relations between entities. More specifically, verbs profile processes, which are complex relations over time.

For example, in sentences 1 through 3, the noun *sister* profiles a human female; *bought* and *sold* are both verbs, which, by definition, profile processes (in this case, the transfer of an item between owners) and their related constituent entities.

Verbs also include an additional conceptual component, as we saw in examples 1 through 3: a prominence asymmetry between the entities participating in a specific relation. Although the event itself and all three entities are profiled (against a background domain of economic transfer) by both *bought* and *sold,* the difference in their construals is based on which entity serves as the primary figure. "Semantically encoded entities are correlated with different degrees of importance; certain elements are more prominent than others since they are most salient in the speaker's mind and call for more attention on the part of the listener" (Shibatani 1985, 832).

In Cognitive Grammar the primary figure in a relation is referred to as the *trajector,* and the secondary figure is called the *landmark.* The trajector of *bought* is the buyer, whereas the trajector of *sold* is the seller. The landmark of both verbs is the item that changes hands. The verbs *bought* and *sold* actually profile three entities as participants within the event, so the additional entity is a secondary landmark; the majority of verbs profile two entities—one trajector and one landmark—along with the process in which they are involved.

The trajector of a multivalent verb is prototypically an agent or actor, and the landmark is prototypically the patient or recipient of the action. The prominence asymmetries in trajector/landmark distinctions serve as the basis for Cognitive Grammar definitions of grammatical relations like subject and object. When used in active voice in declarative sentences, as in example sentences 1 and 2, the nominal used to elaborate the trajector of a verb is the subject, which is correspondingly the most prominent grammatical position (Wolfart 1991; Croft 2005; Goldberg 2006). The nominal that elaborates a verb's landmark is the grammatical object.

In example sentence 1 the trajector of *bought* is the buyer, so the focus is on *Scott,* expressed in subject position, which is the most prominent grammatical position. The item exchanged (i.e., "the painting") has secondary prominence since it is expressed as the direct object, while the seller (i.e., "my sister") is third because it is expressed as an oblique. The verb *sold* profiles the seller as the trajector and thus evokes a different construal. In sentence 2 the entities are expressed in a different order, and the relative prominence of their grammatical positions evokes a construal with the focus on the seller rather than the buyer. These same aspects of prominence asymmetry underlie the differences in construal between active and passive sentences, as exemplified by sentence 3.

THE ENGLISH PASSIVE CONSTRUCTION

The form of the passive construction in English consists of a subject nominal naming the patient of the root verb, a form of *to be*, the past participle of a transitive root verb, and an optional oblique *by*-phrase with a nominal naming the agent of the root verb.

As discussed earlier with the multivalent verbs *bought* and *sold*, the valence of a verb is the number of participants in the event that it semantically encodes (Talmy 2000). Divalent verbs encode a relation and its two participants. The trajector of a divalent verb is prototypically an agent or actor, and the landmark is prototypically the patient or recipient of the action. In the active-voice sentence in example 4, the divalent verb *made* profiles an abstract "maker" as trajector and, as landmark, some object that was made:

4.   Sally made dinner.

Figure 2.1 is a diagram of the divalent verb *make* based on Langacker's (1991) notation. The trajector, in this case a generic "maker," is represented by the upper circle, labeled *tr*. The landmark, here the "object made," is represented by the lower circle labeled *lm*. The arrow in the middle represents the relation between the two entities. Both circles and

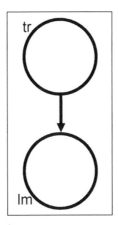

FIGURE 2.1. Diagram of *make*.

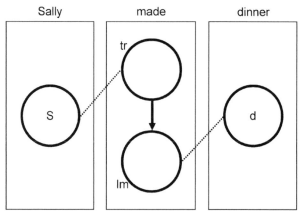

FIGURE 2.2. Diagram of "Sally made dinner."

the arrow are presented in bold to show that the trajector, landmark, and relation are all profiled.

A verb alone does not specify what entities will serve as its trajector and landmark. Verbs combine with other arguments to create sentences. Once again we see that meaning and form go hand in hand because the semantic roles correlate with specific grammatical positions as well:

> Choice of subject and object (and as we see shortly, also obliques), is largely relative: The subject must act on the object in some way (physical or otherwise).
>
> . . . when any force-dynamic relationship is expressed by a simple active transitive verb, the assignment of participants as subject and object is clear: The initiator is the subject and the endpoint is the object. (Croft 1998, 82–83)

In the active sentence shown in example 4, the noun *Sally* in subject position elaborates the trajector of the verb *made*, and through their correspondence the addressee correctly understands that Sally is the "maker." The noun *dinner* in object position elaborates the landmark of *made*, establishing a semantic correspondence to express that the object made in this case was "dinner." Figure 2.2 shows a representation of example 4 in simplified Langacker notation.[1]

1. Full notations following Langacker also include the representation of tense. Since tense does not affect the profile asymmetries that allow for defocused agents and constitute the active/passive distinction, semantic representations of tense are not included in notations throughout this book.

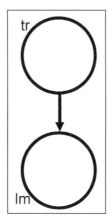

FIGURE 2.3. Diagram of a divalent verb.

The form of the verb in English passive constructions is not the same as that used in active sentences; in passive constructions the verb is inflected as a past participle. The particular form used in passives is described by Langacker (1991, 2002) as PERF3, which puts the primary focus on the patient; thus, the landmark of the root verb is the trajector of the past participle form PERF3. It is this choice of the root verb's landmark as PERF3's trajector that allows the English passive construction to carry out its primary pragmatic function of defocusing the agent. Figure 2.3 shows a diagram of a schematic divalent verb; for comparison, figure 2.4 shows the composite of the PERF3 form of a divalent verb.

In the passive sentence in example 5, the PERF3 form *made* is used, profiling the landmark of *make* as its trajector. The trajector of the PERF3 verb is elaborated by *dinner* in subject position, so the addressee

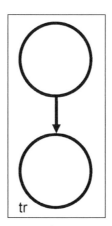

FIGURE 2.4. Diagram of a PERF3 verb.

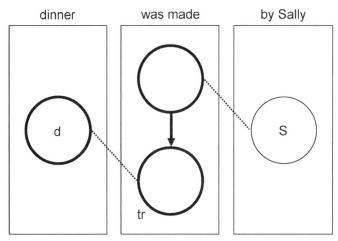

FIGURE 2.5. Diagram of "Dinner was made by Sally."

understands that the dinner is the object made. In this case, the utterance includes a *by*-phrase overtly naming the agent as well; it is elaborated in an oblique prepositional phrase informing the addressee that Sally is the "maker" of the dinner. Figure 2.5 shows example 5 in composite form.

5. Dinner was made by Sally.

The PERF3 form of the verb in the English passive construction highlights the patient as its trajector. As a verb it profiles a complex relation and the entities involved in it. The circles representing each entity and the arrow representing the relation between them are all shown in bold in figure 2.5 to indicate this profiling. The agent of *make*, though profiled within the semantics of the verb, is not the trajector and is thus defocused relative to the patient.

In addition to the relatively low level of prominence given to the agent within the verb's profile structure, the vast majority of instances of passive constructions, in English as well as cross-linguistically, do not overtly mention the agent (Jespersen 1924; Svartvik 1966; Goldberg 2005; Marín-Arrese 2008). Even though the agent is semantically present, as a secondary entity in the profile of the PERF3 verb, the lack of overt specification serves to defocus it even further. In those passives that do include overt expression of the agent, it is expressed as an oblique and thus has "the lowest degree of focus among the syntactically encoded elements" (Shibatani 1985, 833). When no *by*-phrase is included, as in the majority of passive utterances, the evoked construal is one in which the agent is defocused to its fullest extent because it is both removed from prominence and left unspecified. When a *by*-phrase is included, the agent is construed with a reduced level of focus relative to both the other entities in the utterance and its canonical construal in an active-voice utterance. The agent is specified in the utterance but in a position of low prominence, resulting in a reduced-focus construal.

In summary, the English passive construction invokes a construal in which the agent of a transitive verb is defocused. This defocusing is the result of a lack of both grammatical prominence and semantic specificity. The agent is expressed with a relatively low level of focus due to the profile structure of the PERF3 verb. This verb form semantically profiles an entity other than the agent (namely, the patient) as trajector and signals a noncanonical relationship between semantic roles. This semantic structure is overtly encoded in the grammatical structure through the expression of the patient as the subject, the most syntactically prominent position. The majority of passive utterances also lack specification of the agent because the agent's identity is not overtly identified, resulting in further defocusing of the agent. If the agent is overtly specified, it is expressed as an adjunct, a less prominent syntactic position.

DEFOCUSING AGENTS: PROMINENCE AND SPECIFICITY

The construal of the level of focus on a given entity is based on its relative prominence and specificity. In English (and other agent-oriented languages), subject position has the highest degree of prominence of any position within a sentence (Shibatani 1985; Wolfart 1991; Croft 2005; Goldberg 2006), so an entity expressed in subject position is understood to be in primary focus. It makes sense, then, that one of the main ways to defocus the agent of a two-participant event, cross-linguistically, is to use a passive construction (Goldberg 2005).

The construal difference inherent in the passive/active distinction is based on the relative levels of prominence and specification, but passive constructions are not the only symbolic units that encode relatively low prominence or specificity. "[L]anguage provides various morphosyntactic means of distributing, among the semantically coded elements, the focus strength correlated with the amount of attention required" (Shibatani 1985, 832). The passive construction is one, but certainly not the only, linguistic defocusing strategy. The analysis of ASL structures that construe

Construction Type	Example Utterance	Status of the Agent	
		Prominent	Specific
active voice	**Sally** stole your bicycle.	+	+
active voice with impersonal pronoun subject	**Someone** stole your bicycle.	+	<
passive voice with a *by*-phrase	Your bicycle was stolen by **Sally**.	<	+
passive voice with a *by*-phrase containing an impersonal pronoun	Your bicycle was stolen by **someone**.	<	<
passive voice without a *by*-phrase	Your bicycle was stolen.	—	—

the agent at various levels of focus is a search not for a passive syntactic structure in ASL but rather for the particular syntactic structures that ASL users employ as agent-defocusing strategies.

The lack of overt expression of the agent in most passive utterances is an extension of defocusing through low levels of both specification and prominence. In fact, the two dimensions interact:

> A participant not accorded its usual focal prominence (e.g., a passive agent) often remains unspecified. Conversely, failure to provide specific information about a participant renders it less salient. Absence of focal prominence and absence of specificity are mutually reinforcing strategies of defocusing. (Langacker 2006, 130)

It is possible to understand all of the strategies for reducing focus on the agent, including passive constructions, as various points on a spectrum of agent focus with the level of agent focus evoked by each form based on the interactions between prominence and specificity. Consider the examples in table 2.1.

All of the sentences in table 2.1 use a form of the verb *steal*. *Steal* encodes the process in which an item is taken away from its owner without permission. This process is a divalent relation between the item that was taken and the person who took it. The identity of the original owner of the item is not required to be overtly expressed, though it is often included as a possessive determiner, as is the case with the word *your*. Consider the examples in table 2.1.

The first sentence in the chart, *Sally stole your bicycle*, is in active voice. In active constructions, the agent is semantically specified as an overt nominal (labeled as +specific in table 2.1) and grammatically prominent in subject position (+prominent in table 2.1). This combination evokes an agent-focused construal. In a passive construction without a *by*-phrase, such as the final sentence in table 2.1 (*Your bicycle was stolen*), the agent lacks prominence (–prominent) and lacks specificity (–specific), evoking a defocused agent construal.

There are several possible intermediate levels of agent focus as well. When a *by*-phrase is present in a passive construction, the agent is specified (+prominent), but its position in an oblique rather than as the subject gives it reduced grammatical prominence (Croft 2005) (labeled as <prominent in table 2.1). Following this same analysis, expressing an agent as an indefinite pronoun evokes it with reduced specificity (<specific). Pronouns like *one, some, everybody, anybody,* and so on exemplify the generic and vague sense of the agent that such indefinite pronouns provide. An agent thus evoked can occur as either the subject of an active utterance (+prominent) or in an oblique *by*-phrase (–prominent) in a passive utterance. In both cases the agent has less focus than in an active sentence with a fully specified agent, but the passive utterance combines lack of prominence with lack of specificity, resulting in an even further defocusing of the agent.

OTHER TYPES OF LINGUISTIC DEFOCUSING: IMPERSONALIZATION STRATEGIES

Emphasis on the function of passive constructions as a defocusing strategy allows for correlations between passives and other impersonal forms both in English and cross-linguistically (Shibatani 1985; Kemmer 1993; Goldberg 1995; Marín-Arrese 2008). Awareness of the variety of forms that encode a defocused construal allows for a more thorough description of defocused agent expressions in ASL. Shibatani (1985) explains several forms of defocusing, including the use of case marking, indefinite (as opposed to definite) forms, and plural rather than singular. Marín-Arrese (2008) describes impersonal forms in English such as indefinite pronouns, generic-reference pronouns, existentials, and nominalizations. Through a relative lack of specificity and prominence asymmetry similar to that seen in the English passive construction, each of these linguistic forms can reduce focus on the agent, though to varying degrees.

Strategies for reducing focus also include nominalization, existentials, and infinitives. Recall that verbs encode relations that are "*conceptually dependent,* in the sense that their conception presupposes and incorporates the conception of their participants" (Langacker 2006, 116; italics in the original). Divalent verbs profile the relationship itself and both of the entities involved, but other forms impose different types of profiling onto the same event. In nominalizations of divalent verbs, "the actional component is obscured, and the event is presented as an 'abstract thing'" (Marín-Arrese 2008, 446). Through conceptual reification the profile shifts from the relation and its participating entities to "one instance of the event designated by the verb" (Langacker 2006, 119). Infinitive verbs shift the profile to the relation only, leaving the entities involved unprofiled. Marín-Arrese (2008) also categorizes existentials (e.g., *there is . . . , there are . . .*) as an impersonalization strategy because they offer a "non-causal, non-eventive construal" (446), which necessarily abstracts away from concept of a causal agent.

English speakers also use the "inclusive *we*" impersonally as a defocused agent pronoun because it refers to "an incompletely defined collectivity that includes the speaker and one or more others, without specifying who they are" (Kitagawa and Lehrer 1990, 745). Other personal pronouns (e.g., *you, they*) may be used without a specified referent to create this same generic or uncertain sense due to the fact that they reduce the addressee's ability to identify the participant(s) (Langacker 2000).

All of the impersonalization strategies discussed earlier, including the passive construction, can thus be understood as evoking a particular level of focus on the agent as a result of the combination of prominence and specificity. This understanding of the interaction between prominence and specificity is crucial to the analysis of the ASL elicited data, where the issue of nonovertly expressed entities becomes even more important.

THE ASL DATA

An understanding of how ASL expresses construals in which agents are defocused provides unique insights into the relationships between form and meaning and the construals shared by signers/speakers and addressees. Cross-linguistic research has shown that the primary function of passive constructions is to defocus the agent, most often not even mentioning the agent overtly (Jespersen 1924; Svartvik 1966; Goldberg 2005; Marín-Arrese 2008).

In order to determine what constructions exist in ASL to encode defocused agent construals, I elicited data from native ASL users in response to three different types of prompts: twenty individual passive sentences in English; four narrative texts in English, each containing multiple passive constructions; and a video of an ASL description of the process of making pencils (to elicit an ASL-to-English translation).

Four deaf participants completed the elicitation task. The participants were specifically selected because they all have native proficiency in ASL and advanced English reading and writing skills and are able to discuss the metalinguistic aspects of their own language use. The participants' parents are deaf, and they were brought up in homes where ASL was used as the primary language even before they were born. All four have participated in advanced, postsecondary education, which attests to their level of fluency in written English. Additionally, all of the participants have been involved in research projects and have worked in educational environments in which linguistic and metalinguistic awareness of both ASL and English are critical. All of these factors made them ideal participants for this type of elicitation.

Because the task was translation, it was not expected that all of the participants would choose the exact same structure for their responses. For example, when translating a prompt sentence that contains an overt *by*-phrase naming the agent, signers could potentially produce any of several of possible structures in ASL. They might produce a parallel structure with the agent specified in a location in the sentence that reduces its prominence, such as in object position or in an oblique. They could produce an utterance with the agent specified in subject position, giving it primary focus, thus effectively changing the construal to be more analogous to an active construction. Another possibility would be to produce an utterance in which the agent was unstated and therefore unspecified and nonprominent, resulting in a construal that puts no focus on the agent. The nature of the translation task allowed the participants to produce a variety of ASL expressions, and the analysis of their choices sheds light on the structural patterns used in ASL to evoke a range of levels of agent focus.

In addition to translation itself allowing for multiple options, the more open-ended elicitation prompts allow for a wider range in how participants construe and express the events presented. Two-participant events can be expressed as either as agent focused or patient focused. Although text prompts provide greater flexibility in terms of participants' sign choices, there is no guarantee that signers will produce agent-defocused forms in their translations. Participants could potentially produce entirely agent-focused ASL expressions in response to such open-ended prompts. Conversely, individual passive sentence prompts in English, although targeted enough to impose a defocused agent construal, could skew the participants' responses toward an English-influenced grammatical order and/or lexical choices. To balance these potential pros and cons, both text translation and isolated sentence translation were included as elicitation methods. The ASL-to-English translation task was also included to determine whether participants consider defocused agent forms in English, particularly the passive construction, as semantically parallel to defocused agent utterances in ASL.

For the analysis of ASL utterances, the most important consideration is the relationship between form and meaning. The data were grouped according to syntactic form, and then each syntactic construction was analyzed to determine the level of agent focus that form evokes. As is true with English examples, a relatively low level of focus can be assigned to entities through the domains of prominence and specificity, and these same factors proved critical in understanding the construals evoked in the ASL data.

Chapter 3

Features Relevant to Agent Focus in ASL

We now turn to issues of ASL syntax relevant to the analysis of structures that impact the level of focus on agents in ASL. We look first at nonovert arguments and then at indicating verbs and surrogates. Since these features influence the level of focus on entities in ASL utterances, the concepts introduced in this section are vital for our understanding of the following chapters.

Several aspects of ASL grammar impinge on the ways that we mentally structure concepts and meaning. For example, previous research has shown that ASL utterances do not require overt subjects when the agent's identity is recoverable due to its salience in the preceding discourse (Liddell 2003). The analysis of defocused agent constructions I present in this book suggests that nonovert subject utterances are not limited to situations in which agents are recoverable; they are also readily used when the agent is unrecoverable, with the effect of achieving a specific discourse purpose: defocusing the agent. The interaction between the grammatical structure of utterances without overt subjects and an addressee's ability to recover and/or identify the agentive entity results in various levels of focus on the agent.

Another interesting aspect of signed languages that relates to the construed level of focus on an entity is the intimate relation with physical space, not just for sign production but also for conceptual blending (Liddell 2003). Examples can be seen in the use of indicating verbs, which must be directed toward at least one referent, and surrogate blends in which the signer is understood to be physically representing an event participant rather than performing the narrative role. Generally, referents that are not physically present are identified overtly and mapped onto an area of the signing space prior to being referenced with an indicating verb or incorporated into a surrogate blend (Baker and Cokely 1980; Mikos, Smith, and Lentz 2001; Liddell 1995, 2003).[1]

---

1. Liddell's work introduced the terms *indicating verb* and *surrogate blend*; prior to this these entities were most often called "agreement verbs" and "role shifting," respectively.

The research findings presented here have significant implications for this previously understood "requirement" to overtly identify referents mapped onto the signing space. The data show that even when using indicating verbs and surrogate blends, signers may choose to defocus the agent for pragmatic reasons. To do so, they leave the agent's identity unstated, resulting in a prominent, visually evoked agent within the verb, which is simultaneously defocused by a lack of overt lexical specificity in the clause. Let us review the relevant aspects of the use of space in ASL as previously described in the literature, so that their influence on semantic structuring can be better understood.

NONOVERT ARGUMENTS

The most prevalent form of defocused agent utterances in the elicited ASL data are clauses that lack an overt subject. Earlier research has argued for the grammatical acceptability of subjectless clauses based on appropriate discourse conditions. Specifically, ASL allows nonovert subjects and/or objects when the entity is salient in the discourse, either through topicalization or prior mention (Liddell 2003). Divalent verbs by definition include both a trajector and a landmark in their profile; however, in ASL, that trajector and/or the landmark need not be overtly elaborated when they correspond to an entity already salient in the discourse.

1. PRO-1 SELL POSS-1 CAR[2]
   I sold my car.

   _____t
2. POSS-1 CAR PRO-1 SELL
   My car, I sold it.

The utterance in example 1 contains the verb SELL, which profiles the "seller" as trajector and the "object sold" as landmark. The trajector of SELL is elaborated in example 1 by PRO-1 in subject position, overtly identifying the addressee as the "seller." Similarly, the landmark of SELL is elaborated by the noun phrase POSS-1 CAR, overtly identifying the "object sold" as the addressee's car.

The utterance in example 2, in contrast, begins with the topicalized noun phrase POSS-1 CAR, which makes the addressee's car salient in the

2. Examples 1–3 are from Liddell (2003, 63).

discourse. The topic is followed by the main clause, which includes both the pronoun PRO-1 and the verb SELL. As in example 1, the trajector of SELL is elaborated by PRO-1, identifying the addressee as the "seller"; however, in example 2, nothing follows the verb to elaborate it. In this case, the addressee is responsible for selecting an entity in the discourse as the "object sold." Since the addressee's car was recently made salient in the discourse, it is straightforward for the addressee to select the addressee's car as the object that was sold even though the car is unspecified and not prominent within the clause.

Topicalization, as demonstrated by example 2, is one way that an entity can be made salient in the discourse; another way is through previous mention. If the sentence in example 3 were uttered in response to a question about what had happened to the addressee's old car, the addressee would understand the "object sold" to be the car even though there is no syntactic object produced in the sentence itself to elaborate the landmark of SELL. In this case, the question would provide the discourse salience to the car despite its lack of prominence in the response.

3. PRO-1 SELL
   I sold it.

A further example in which a subject rather than an object is not overtly mentioned is Liddell's example 39 (2003, 59), reproduced here as example 4, given as a brief response to someone who noticed that a particular boy was limping and asked what had happened. In this case it is not necessary to sign the subject, BOY, overtly because the question has already made the limping boy salient in the discourse.

4. FALL
   He fell down.

A major finding of the research presented in this book is that an entity can be profiled as trajector and not overtly elaborated even when it is not already salient in the discourse. When this happens, the construal evoked is one in which the agent is defocused. The ability of addressees to glean the appropriate semantic contribution of trajectors and landmarks of verbs when they are not elaborated lexically is central to the discussion of non-agent-focused forms in ASL. The elicited ASL data analyzed in chapters 4 and 5 suggest that signers leave agents unexpressed even when producing isolated utterances where there is no previous discourse context. The narrative data in chapters 6 and 7 show how signers use the interaction between discourse-level salience and utterance-level prominence to adjust the relative levels of focus on multiple entities, thereby maintaining coherence within the narrative.

CONCEPTUAL BLENDING

When we get to the data descriptions, we will see that the elicited ASL utterances with nonovert subjects remove focus from the agent by not expressing it. Recall from the discussion of *bought* and *sold*, however, that the prominence asymmetry between trajector and landmark is not determined by word-order issues alone; the asymmetrical profile structure is inherent in the meaning of the verbs themselves. As we analyze the level of agent focus in a given utterance, it is important to consider the semantic content of the verb in addition to the lexical constituents of the utterance. In ASL, verbs can be divided into different categories based on their semantic content; the distinction of relevance to the issue of agent prominence is that between those that include conceptual blending and those that do not.

As part of linguistic utterances in ASL, conceptual blending allows for discourse elements to be depicted by using parts of the body, face, and hands (Liddell 2003). For example, an ASL user might choose to represent the image in figure 3.1, as the signer does in figure 3.2, namely, by producing the nominal BICYCLE followed by a conceptually blended depiction of the scene. In this case, the signer places her right hand vertically to represent the bicycle in an upright position and her left hand flat and oriented horizontally to represent the surface on which the bicycle is parked (figure 3.2).

Depiction, conceptually blending the physical articulators (hands, arms, face, and body) with conceived entities, is often used in ASL discourse.

FIGURE 3.1. A parked bicycle.

FIGURE 3.2. The sign BICYCLE followed by a depiction of a bicycle.

The blending may range from relatively straightforward examples, like the depiction of a stationary bicycle, to complex, multilayered blends of events occurring over time. When signers express complex events, they conceptualize the scene and make choices about how and whether to depict various entities, their spatial relationships, their movements and interactions, and (in the case of human or anthropomorphized entities) even their emotional and mental reactions to one another (Liddell 2003; Dudis 2002, 2004).

Signers' conceptualization of events includes the entities involved as well as their relative locations. In the depiction of events, the space around the signer is blended with the space in which the depicted event occurred. For example, Liddell (2003, 160–62) describes an event in which a girl is depicted as walking ahead of her two younger sisters. The signer extends his right index finger upward to depict a single person and extends the first two fingers of his left hand upward to depict two people standing together. He then places his right hand ahead and to the right of the left and moves both hands forward, depicting the movement of the three girls and their spatial locations relative to each other.

SURROGATE BLENDS

Signers may also depict a scene by blending themselves with an entity in the event and depicting that entity's actions. In the same narrative (Liddell 2003, 160–62), after the relative locations of the sisters have been established, the signer points to his right to indicate the conceptually blended location where the older sister was previously depicted. After producing this pronominal to serve as a referent, he then turns his face, eye gaze, and body to the left, conceptually blending himself with the older sister in the story and demonstrating her looking at her younger sisters, who were placed in the blended space to the left of the older sister. The signer is understood to be conceptually blended with the older sister, and the empty space to the signer's left as conceptually blended with the younger sisters. Because the signer and/or a specific space is understood to represent an entity in the event, Liddell (2003) refers to this type of conceptual blending as *surrogate blending*.[3]

The conceptual blending involved in surrogate blending is important to the analysis of defocused agents in ASL. The data show that surrogate blends depicting the actions of agents can be used even in utterances that do not contain overt subjects. In such utterances, the signers are understood to be depicting the surrogate agent's action, but the agent's identity is unspecified because a referent was not previously established within the conceptual blend. Because the agent is unspecified, its prominence is diminished despite the fact that it is visible as the actor in the surrogate blend.

INDICATING VERBS

In addition to the use of surrogate blending to depict actions, a specific class of ASL verbs takes advantage of conceptual blending; these verbs are directed toward the referents involved in the event they encode. These verbs have been described in several different ways in the literature on signed language linguistics, most notably as agreement verbs (based on Padden 1988) and as indicating verbs (based on Liddell 2000). Since Liddell's analysis utilizes cognitive linguistic principles, I followed his terminology for discussions of this verb class here and throughout this book.

In indicating verbs, the movement and orientation parameters of the sign can be meaningfully directed to indicate the referent intended as the elaboration of their trajector and/or landmark. Indicating verbs may be directed toward two types of entities: those that are present at the time of the utterance and those that are not present but for which locations are

3. This particular way of using the signing space has been described in various ways in the literature, including role-shift (Loew 1983), referential shift (Emmorey 1994), constructed action (Metzger 1994), and shifted referential framework (Morgan 1999), among others.

mapped onto the signing space through conceptual blending. When the entities involved in an event described by a particular utterance are present, a signer can meaningfully direct an indicating verb so that it points to or moves toward the intended referent. The addressee understands that the present referent is meant to elaborate the trajector and/or landmark of that verb. When the referent corresponding to an indicating verb's trajector or landmark is not present during the utterance, conceptual blending is used to depict the location of intended referents in the signing space. Once the mapped locations have been established, the signer can meaningfully direct an indicating verb so that it points to or moves toward the mapped location, and the addressee will understand that the mapped referent is meant to elaborate the trajector and/or landmark of that verb.

In later chapters we will see that the elicited ASL data contain instances of indicating verbs used even in utterances that do not contain overt subjects. Perhaps somewhat surprisingly, the participants readily use verbs that indicate a space to map onto the trajector in utterances for which no entity has been conceptually established in that location. In these cases, though the agent is indicated in the phonology of the verb itself, giving it some prominence, the identity of the agent is unspecified and therefore reduced in focus.

PREVIOUS RESEARCH ON PASSIVE VOICE IN ASL

While several previous studies (Stokoe, Casterline, and Croneberg 1965; Wilbur 1987; Isenhath 1990; Kegl 1990) have discussed whether specific forms in ASL can be analyzed as passive, the most in-depth look at agent-defocused constructions in ASL to date is Janzen, O'Dea, and Shaffer's (2001) "The Construal of Events: Passives in American Sign Language." As their title suggests, Janzen et al. take an approach based on pragmatics and function and determine that certain constructions in ASL are indeed passive. Their definition of the prototypical passive in ASL is a construction that contains these characteristics:

1. Defocusing, or the demotion of the agent, so that the agent is not mentioned . . .

2. The event is viewed from the patient's perspective rather than the agent's . . .

3. For a transitive agreement verb, defocusing the agent so that the agent is not mentioned means that, rather than specifying an agent in the syntax by associating an agent NP with a particular locus, the locus is empty . . . in the passive construction, no agent is specified, with the result that the movement of the agreement verb begins at a morphosyntactic, but semantically empty, locus. (289–90)

The descriptions and analyses given by Janzen et al. (2001) are directly applicable to some of the data presented here. This data set was elicited in response to prompts that specifically defocused the agent, so Janzen et al.'s first characteristic of prototypical passives, namely, that the agent is defocused, is true of the vast majority of the examples in the current data as well. In a few instances, signers added an explicit agent and/or increased focus on the agent in their utterance; those constructions were therefore more similar to prototypical active constructions than to passives.

Because Janzen et al. (2001) sought to determine whether passive and active forms could be distinguished in ASL and, if so, what the prototypical passive form consists of, they focused on indicating verbs (those that are meaningfully directed in space, which they call "transitive agreement verbs").[4] In the present study the analysis is not limited to those utterances that may be passive in ASL; rather, I analyze a variety of utterances used to defocus the agent. Because my goal is to determine what forms are used to express meanings in which the agent is defocused and/or reduced in focus relative to active-voice clauses, the type of verb was purposely not controlled. Indicating verbs similar to those that Janzen et al. studied make up only a small subset of the data elicited for the current analysis; the specific examples are discussed in chapter 5.

For indicating verbs the question of whether the signer has taken the perspective of the patient or the agent (the second characteristic of prototypical ASL passive constructions according to Janzen et al.) is relevant. The elicited data contain remarkably few utterances with indicating verbs produced from the patient's perspective, as in the examples given by Janzen et al. (2001); the utterances that do utilize indicating verbs are predominantly given from a narrative perspective in which the signers do not identify themselves with either the agent or the patient.

As noted in Janzen et al.'s third characteristic of prototypical passives, when an indicating verb is produced without overt mention of the agent

---

4. I follow Liddell (1995, 2000, 2003) and refer to these as "indicating verbs."

(or, indeed, of the patient), the beginning and/or ending locations of the verb in signing space are mapped onto referents that are left unspecified. As I further discuss with the specific examples in later chapters, the current analysis suggests that signers use signing space to indicate referents regardless of whether those referents are specified within the utterance, specified previously in the discourse, or, most important for the discussion of defocused agents, never overtly specified at all.

The major difference between the current study and previous work on this topic is that this study takes the construal invoked by passive constructions as its starting point. Rather than attempting to determine the form of a passive construction in ASL, the research question here is, how does ASL express construals in which the agent is not the primary entity in focus? Instead of seeing passives as the overarching category and these ASL structures as a subgroup within that category, agent-defocused structures are taken as a broad category into which a passive construction would fall. The goal is not to search for passives but rather to identify utterances that defocus the agent and describe them. The next logical linguistic step—attempting to determine whether those ASL utterances are passive and constitute a construction—is an adjacent theme that I discuss briefly in the concluding chapter.

SUMMARY AND CONCLUSION

In order to determine the structures ASL signers use to express a semantic equivalent of the English passive, one must first understand the pragmatic function of passive constructions. Previous cross-linguistic research has shown that the primary function of passive constructions is to defocus the agent, most often not even mentioning the agent overtly. For the current analysis of the elicited ASL data, the most important consideration is how the agent is construed. A relatively low level of focus can be assigned to entities through the domains of prominence and specificity, which in turn are closely tied to nonovert expression of agents in the ASL data. Because ASL allows for nonovert agents and patients in certain discourse situations not limited to the function of defocusing, special attention was paid to the sentence structure, use of space to refer to entities, and the overt expression (or omission) of arguments.

Although these issues are somewhat controversial in the ASL linguistics literature, addressing them from the starting point of how ASL expresses construals in which agents are defocused provides unique insights into the relationships between form and meaning and the understood construals shared by signers/speakers and addressees. It also serves as an advanced starting point for potential future research related to the development of classroom materials for both ASL and English L2 environments and for interpreters working with both languages.

Chapter 4

Defocused Agents in ASL Utterances

Chapters 4 and 5 present my analysis of agent focus in ASL utterances elicited as translations of individual passive sentence prompts from English. The elicited ASL translations include a variety of utterance types. As discussed in chapter 2, the level of focus on an entity depends on both the specificity with which it is expressed and the prominence it is given within the syntactic structure. As we will see, ASL users have at their disposal a range of constructions that vary in the level of focus with which they construe the agent, which reflects both its degree of prominence and its degree of specificity.

Because our understanding of language is based on the connection between form and meaning, this analysis follows those two interrelated aspects. The first step was to determine the structural form of the ASL utterances, and the second step was to analyze their meaning. In this way, various constructions were identified, each with a unique syntactic form that construes the agent with a certain level of focus.

The various ASL constructions that appear in the elicited data are here categorized according to three main levels of agent focus: utterances that express a construal with the agent fully in focus; utterances that express defocused agent construals; and utterances that express a reduced agent focus construal, which are described in chapter 5.

In any discussion of language data, one must understand where the data come from, so I first provide an overview of the prompt materials.

COLLECTION OF ENGLISH-TO-ASL SENTENCE TRANSLATIONS

Twenty passive sentences in English were presented one at a time to deaf adult native ASL users who were asked to translate the sentences into ASL (table 4.1). The sentences were adapted from textbook and website materials designed for teaching the passive construction to English language learners.

TABLE 4.1. *English Sentence Prompts.*

1	Your bicycle was damaged in the accident.
2	I have never been beaten at chess.
3	That old car will never be stolen.
4	This street has been closed because of the snow.
5	Peter wasn't invited to the party.
6	German is spoken in Austria.
7	The best cars are made in Japan.
8	The report must be completed by next Friday.
9	His bike is being repaired.
10	Receipts should be given to the secretary tomorrow.
11	I am encouraged by the positive results.
12	Rachel was brought to this country from Africa as a slave.
13	She is believed to have lived in Virginia for a short time.
14	Our project needs to be completed before her new book gets published.
15	His car was being repaired, so he asked his friend for a ride to work.
16	Dinner is going to be made by Sally tonight.
17	Rules were made to be broken.
18	Ice has been discovered on Mars.
19	The recommendation was vetoed by the president.
20	The results will be published in the newspaper tomorrow.

Although the primary consideration for all of these sentences was that the main verb be expressed in a passive construction, additional features related to defocusing were also purposely included in the set to elicit as wide a variety of responses as possible. For example, sentence 14 contains two passive clauses ("needs to be completed" and "gets published"), sentence 17 includes a passive infinitive ("to be broken"), and the subject of sentence 19 is a nominalization[1] of a transitive event ("recommendation"). While most of the verbs are divalent, meaning that they encode the relationship between two entities, one passive construction is trivalent; the trivalent verb *given,* which occurs in sentence 10, encodes the relationship between an unnamed giver, an object given, and a receiver. Three of the passive verbs occur in modal constructions (the modals are *must, should,* and *needs to*).

1. Recall from chapter 2 that infinitives and nominalizations with transitive root verbs are impersonalization strategies in English, so they are included here as a defocused agent form. As I show later, the way the participants expressed the events in ASL translations also warrants their inclusion here.

The primary discourse function of passive voice is to defocus the agent (Shibatani 1985), and the vast majority of instances of passive constructions, in English and cross-linguistically, do not overtly mention the agent (Jespersen 1924; Svartvik 1966; Goldberg 2005; Marín-Arrese 2008). Eighteen of the twenty-one passive verbs are in sentences without a *by*-phrase, so they have no overt nominal naming the agent. Three sentences with *by*-phrases (sentences 11, 16, and 19) were included in order to determine whether signers would choose an active expression rather than an agent-defocused expression when the agent is known.

ANALYSIS OF ENGLISH-TO-ASL SENTENCE TRANSLATIONS

The elicitation task resulted in video data of each of the four participants' ASL translations of the twenty passive sentences from English. The ASL data were glossed and labeled using ELAN video annotation software, which is freely available through the Language Archiving Portal at Max Planck Institute (http://www.lat-mpi.eu/tools/elan/).

In order to analyze the relationship between the semantics and the syntax of the ASL utterances, the semantic properties of each ASL verb produced were considered, following definitions from Langacker (1987). In cognitive grammar, verbs profile processes, which are complex relations over time. Each sign that encoded a profiled process (an event or temporal relation) was identified as a verb and then analyzed to determine its valence properties. The verbs were divided into the following categories: zero valence, monovalent (one-entity event), divalent (two-entity event), trivalent (three-entity event), adjectival or depicting predication, or affect verb.

The main goal was to determine whether each utterance included an overtly expressed agent, so for each verb encoding a multivalent event, I analyzed the other signs in the utterance to determine whether the trajector was overtly elaborated and, if so, where in the syntactic structure the elaborating expression occurred. Verbs encoding single-entity events and zero-valence verbs were not included in the analysis.

The analysis of ASL syntactic structure used cognitive grammar definitions of grammatical categories and grammatical relations (Langacker 1987), following Liddell's (2003) application of these definitions to ASL. If the nonmanual signals associated with topicalization (Liddell 1980; Baker-Shenk and Cokely 1980) (i.e., raised eyebrows and/or a backward head tilt or pulling of the head backward) co-occurred with certain signs and marked them as distinct from the declarative portion of the sentence, the signs produced during the nonmanual marking were labeled as topics. Unmarked noun phrases (i.e., those produced without accompanying nonmanual signals) that preceded verbs were labeled as subjects. Unmarked noun phrases immediately following verbs were labeled as objects. Other types of phrases, including adverbials (e.g., TOMORROW, NEXT FRIDAY, NEVER), prepositional phrases (e.g., IN ACCIDENT, #BY FRIDAY, IN VIRGINIA), and discourse markers (e.g., FINISH, FINE), were treated as adjuncts. In some of the sentences, adverbs were expressed before the verb. In several cases, rhetorical questions were used, marked by raised eyebrows and an overt *wh*-question produced midsentence and immediately answered by the signer (Baker-Shenk and Cokely 1980). These were labeled specifically as rhetorical questions, and the utterance that functioned to answer to the rhetorical question was treated as an additional adjunct specific to the rhetorical structure.

In addition to the valence properties, the type of each verb was also labeled so that differences in the uses of plain verbs, indicating verbs, and depicting verbs could be noted. Signs that expressed a process through the depiction of the signer as a participating entity were also labeled to determine the effect of surrogate blending on the relative level of focus on the agent.

Once all of the annotations had been made, the semantic content of each utterance was analyzed to determine whether the agent was expressed overtly. The individual sentences without overtly expressed agents were divided into categories based on their syntactic structures, and frequency rates for each structure were determined.

Table 4.2 shows the breakdown by construal type: agent construed as defocused, agent construed with reduced focus, and agent in focus. The interaction between trajector elaboration and utterance structure results in a range of construals, and the shading in the chart represents this gradation in level of agent focus. Defocused agent construals are shown at the top of the table in the white cells. Utterances that evoke construals that focus on the agent are shown at the bottom of the table in dark gray boxes. I have labeled the midrange construals resulting from the interaction of the utterance structure and trajector elaboration as "reduced agent focus," and they are shown in the middle of the chart with lighter gray shading.

TABLE 4.2. *Construals Expressed in ASL Utterances with Multivalent Verbs.*

Construal	Trajector	Structure: Syntax and Blending	Tokens	Percentage	Total	Total
defocused agent	*not overtly* elaborated	topic verb	39	41%	58 tokens (61%)	71 tokens (75%)
		verb object	19	20%		
reduced agent focus		indicating verbs	10	11%	25 tokens (26%)	
		surrogate blends	3	3%		
		rhetorical structures	6	6%		24 tokens (25%)
	overtly elaborated	underspecified subjects	6	6%		
agent focused		from prompts with *by*-phrases	6	6%	12 tokens (13%)	
		assumed agent expressed overtly	4	4%		
		from active prompt clauses	2	2%		
Total			95	100%		

The main finding was that the ASL utterances express defocused agent construals through the lack of an overtly elaborated trajector. In these constructions, the unstated agent is given no prominence within the utterance and is completely unspecified, therefore defocusing it to the maximum extent possible. As the table shows, the majority of the utterances (61 percent) evoke a defocused agent construal through this lack of an overtly elaborated trajector. These utterances are described later in this chapter.

The data also included a few ASL utterances in which the agent is construed in focus. These have overtly elaborated trajectors that are fully specified and expressed prominently in subject position.

The conclusion that ASL utilizes a range of forms to express construals with varying levels of focus is not problematic in light of the fact that the impersonal forms of English and other spoken languages exhibit a similar variety (Shibatani 1985; Marín-Arrese 2008). In ASL, utterances that do not include overt elaboration of the trajector encode construals that parallel the construals encoded in the range of English impersonal forms, in which prominence and specificity interact to produce reduced agent focus (see table 4.3). Just as English uses a variety of impersonal forms to defocus the agent to differing extents, ASL also has a number of impersonalization strategies based on how agents can be expressed, thus affecting the degree of focus.

Examples of the English construction types were presented in chapter 2, table 2.1. I now consider examples of each of the ASL construction types, grouped according to the level of focus with which each construes the agent. I begin with a brief discussion of utterances that contain overt subjects since that is the canonical position for expressing the agent in focus. Then I turn to the constructions that construe events with the least focus on the agent, and finally I consider all of the in-between examples, where prominence and specificity are interacting to evoke the agent with various levels of focus.

UTTERANCES WITH OVERT SUBJECTS

Multivalent utterances in ASL typically express the agent in subject position. Grammatical position is one of the main ways to linguistically signal relative prominence. In ASL, utterances with overt nominals elaborating both the trajector and the landmark are canonically structured with

TABLE 4.3. *Interaction between Prominence and Specificity in ASL Utterances.*

English Construction Types	ASL Construction Types	Status of the Agent	
		Prominent	Specific
active voice	utterance with overt subject	+	+
active voice with impersonal pronoun subject	utterance with under-specified subject	+	<
passive voice with a *by*-phrase	utterance with agent expressed in rh-question structure	<	+
passive voice with a *by*-phrase containing an impersonal pronoun		<	<
	subjectless utterance with indicating verb	<	—
	subjectless utterance with depicting verb	<	—
passive voice without a *by*-phrase	subjectless utterance with plain verb	—	—

the nominal elaborating the trajector preceding the verb and the nominal elaborating the landmark following the verb, yielding an unmarked subject-verb-object construction. The ASL transitive construction instantiated by utterances of this type is structurally parallel to the English active construction both syntactically and semantically. Expression of the agent as the first unmarked element in the utterance (in subject position) evokes a construal in which the agent is in focus.

For example, one of the ways the participants translated the elicitation sentence "Dinner will be made by Sally tonight." was to alter the construal and produce an agent-focused utterance. The English prompt sentence reduces focus on the agent by using a passive construction with the agent expressed overtly in a *by*-phrase. In the translation (figure 4.1), the nominal s-a-l-l-y is expressed as the overt subject elaborating the trajector of MAKE, and the nominal FOOD is produced as a direct object elaborating the landmark of MAKE. While the English passive sentence encodes a construal of the situation more focused on "dinner" than on "Sally," in the ASL utterance, the agent, "Sally," is overtly specified and grammatically prominent in subject position, resulting in a construal semantically equivalent to the English active sentence "Tonight Sally will make dinner."

TONIGHT   S-A-L-L-Y   MAKE   FOOD
literal translation: "Tonight Sally will make dinner."
FIGURE 4.1. *Utterance with agent in focus.*

Figure 4.2 is a diagram of the semantic structure of the ASL utterance in figure 4.1. The verb MAKE, shown in the box in the center, encodes an event with both a trajector, the "maker," and a landmark, the "thing being made." The trajector is represented by the upper circle in the box, and the landmark is represented by the lower circle; the arrow between them shows the flow of energy between them in the event, which moves from the agentive maker to the object being made. In this ASL utterance, the trajector of MAKE is elaborated by the nominal S-A-L-L-Y, and the landmark of MAKE is elaborated by the nominal FOOD; the dotted lines in the diagram link the trajector and the landmark in the semantics of MAKE to the semantics of the nominals that elaborate them. This same semantic structure is encoded in the English active sentence "Tonight Sally will make dinner."

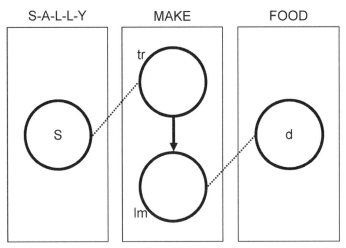

FIGURE 4.2. *Diagram of the utterance in figure 4.1.*

This section describes the ASL syntactic form that results in the most complete defocusing of the agent: subjectless clauses with plain verbs. This is the predominant utterance type in the elicited ASL data, used with 61 percent (58 out of 95) of the tokens of multivalent verbs. These utterances contain multivalent plain verbs, but they do not include an overt elaboration of the trajector, thereby leaving the identity of the agent both unspecified phonologically and nonprominent structurally.

An example of an ASL utterance that contains two of these subjectless clauses was produced in response to the elicitation sentence "Ice has been discovered on Mars" (figure 4.3).

Here the signer uses FIND, which is a divalent verb:

[FIND] is conceptually dependent because it presupposes, as an inherent part of its own internal structure, the two things participating in the correspondences . . . One cannot conceptualize the [FIND] relationship without conceptualizing the two things functioning as trajector and landmark of that relation . . . [FIND] characterizes its trajector and landmark only in schematic terms—the former only as a thing capable of searching and perceiving, the latter only as a thing capable of being found. (Langacker 1988, 104)

< M-A-R-S   index-FAR   depict: 'planet' >topic

FINISH   FIND   HAVE   I-C-E

literal translation: "The planet Mars: . . . discovered . . . there is ice!"

FIGURE 4.3. *Utterance with two verbs evoking defocused agent construal.*

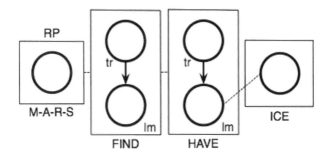

FIGURE 4.4. *Diagram of the utterance in figure 4.3.*

Thus the use of FIND semantically encodes both a "finder" and an "object that was found," as diagrammed in figure 4.4. We know that there must have been a "finder" in order for ice to have been found. In this utterance, however, the trajector of FIND is not overtly elaborated, leaving the identity of the agent who did the finding unstated and thus defocused.

The following clause elaborates the landmark of FIND, and is also an instance of a subjectless construction for which an overtly elaborated agent is not provided. It contains the verb HAVE, which also encodes a trajector and a landmark. The trajector of HAVE is not elaborated; its landmark is elaborated by the nominal I-C-E.

The ASL verb HAVE deserves a bit more discussion. It often occurs without an overt subject and with no identifiable agent recoverable from the previous context. In these subjectless constructions, HAVE seems to function as an existential, informing the addressee of the state of events rather than encoding a possessive relationship. In ASL, subjectless clauses with HAVE can therefore be said to semantically function as existential constructions, analogous to English clauses beginning with "there is/are." This is another example of the use of a nonovert subject form to defocus the agent and produce an impersonalized meaning.[2]

The ASL sentence in figure 4.3 was produced as a translation of the following elicitation sentence:

1. Ice has been discovered on Mars.

2. While the use of subjectless utterances with HAVE as an existential in ASL is not a new idea (e.g., Chen Pichler and Hochgesang 2009), the analysis of it within the framework of agent defocusing and impersonalization strategies is new. Support for this analysis comes from the analysis of the English existential "there is" construction as an impersonalization strategy and from the use of content verbs with "dummy" subjects (e.g., the German *es gibt* construction) for this purpose in other spoken languages.

The topic MARS loc-FAR PLANET serves as a reference point (abbreviated as RP in the diagram in figure 4.2, following Langacker 1991) from which the rest of the sentence should be understood. This leads the addressee to the domain of outer space and therefore to an understanding that "astronauts" or "space scientists" are likely the implied, but unspecified, agent. By providing no overt mention of the agent, the signer produces a sentence that focuses on Mars (as topic) and the discovery that ice exists there rather than on the people who made the discovery.

These nonovert subject utterances, which are so predominant in the elicited ASL data, are structurally quite different from the English passive construction, although both encode a defocused agent construal. The English passive construction is formed by a form of *be* and the past participle of a transitive verb. The patient is expressed in subject position; the agent, if expressed at all, is in an oblique *by*-phrase. The elicited defocused agent expressions in ASL do not contain verb forms that differ from those in ASL agent-focused utterances, nor do they express the patient in subject position. The ASL utterances simply do not contain nominals naming the agent; the verbs in these utterances retain their profile structure (trajector/landmark relationship), and patients are expressed in the same position in which they are found in utterances that do contain overt subjects: either in the direct-object position or as nonmanually marked topics.

Without explicit mention of the agent, these ASL utterances encode the same construal as English passive constructions, namely, defocusing the agent. In the semantic structure, it is the English past participle PERF3 that makes the trajector of the complex passive verb correspond to the landmark of the base transitive verb, thus selecting the patient to be expressed in subject position (Langacker 2000). The ASL data contain no morphological or phonological form marking the verbs as "passive" or causing a shift in trajector (or landmark). For verbs that encode a relation between an agent and a patient, the trajector corresponds to the agent in either case; the only change is in whether that trajector is overtly elaborated. In ASL, signers communicate reduced focus on the agent by using expressions without subject nominals, which leaves the most prominent grammatical position (i.e., subject position) unfilled and the identity of the agent unspecified. This combination of lack of specificity and lack of prominence leads to a construal in which the agent is completely defocused.

Moreover, ASL has been described as allowing for subjectless constructions when an entity can be mapped onto the trajector (Liddell 2003) (i.e., when the identity of the trajector is accessible in the previous discourse).

Embedded within a discourse structure with previously identified entities accessible for mapping onto the trajector, the lack of the focus on
the agent at the sentence level due to the subjectless constructions has
minimal impact because the focused element is readily accessible at the
discourse level. The findings from the current research indicate that this
same type of subjectless utterance, when used without a previously expressed entity accessible for elaboration of the verb's trajector, creates a
semantic structure in which the identity of the trajector is inaccessible.
Thus we can say that, whereas agents are defocused syntactically in English by using forms like the passive construction, they are pragmatically
defocused in ASL by using subjectless constructions for which the verb's
trajector is neither prominent nor specified. I return to this discussion
further in chapter 6, where I discuss ASL translations of texts with agents
expressed at several levels of focus.

Both the agentless English passive construction and the ASL subjectless
construction defocus the agent by leaving it unstated, removing both its
prominence and its specification. On the prominence scale, when a trajector is not elaborated by a nominal, it has no grammatical position in the
utterance, and thus the agent is the least prominent relative to any other
profiled entities in the utterance. On the specificity scale, trajectors that
are not overtly elaborated despite being evoked as part of the semantic
structure of the verb are phonologically unspecified in the utterance. Despite the fact that their syntactic forms are different, the evoked construal
of the events in the subjectless ASL constructions is analogous to the
semantic structure contributed by the English passive-voice construction.

Two different subjectless syntactic structures were used to evoke a
defocused agent construal: utterances with only a topic and a verb and
utterances with a verb followed by an object, both of which are discussed
in this chapter.

Topic-Verb Structure

The form of grammatical structure that occurs most often in the elicited ASL sentences consists of a topicalized nominal followed by a verb.
Thirty-nine of the ninety-five tokens of two- or three-participant events
(41 percent) are expressed using this basic topic-verb structure; they make
up the largest group by far. In most of these utterances, the topicalized
nominal elaborates the landmark of the verb. Several of these utterances
include adjuncts, and some of the sentences contain adverbs or discourse
markers as well. Although this does add some variety to the syntactic
structures produced, the unifying factor is that none of these utterances

< PRO-X.poss   BICYCLE > topic   NOW FIX++
literal translation: "His bicycle: now fix."

FIGURE 4.5. *Defocused agent utterance with topic-verb structure.*

have overt subjects and the trajectors of the verbs are not overtly elaborated. The structure of all of the utterances in this category can be summarized as follows:

"topic-verb" syntactic structure: topic (adverb) verb (adjunct)

One example of an utterance using this topic-verb structural form to evoke a defocused agent construal appears in the response to the elicitation sentence: "His bike is being repaired" (figure 4.5). The signer begins the utterance with the noun phrase PRO-X.poss BICYCLE, which is nonmanually marked as a topic, with eyebrows raised and head tilted backward. The adverb NOW occurs between the topic and the verb FIX.

The verb FIX is divalent, so its semantic structure is similar to the structure of FIND in the previous example. Semantically FIX encodes both a trajector, the agentive "fixer," and a landmark, the "object being fixed." The ASL utterance, however, has no subject, so the trajector of FIX is not overtly elaborated. There is also no object in this clause, which would potentially mean that the landmark of FIX is also unelaborated; however, because BICYCLE was already introduced into the discourse as the topic, it is conceptually available to the addressee and is semantically appropriate to correlate with the "object being fixed." The addressee thus understands that BICYCLE, expressed in a previous clause (in this case, in the preceding topic), elaborates the landmark of the verb FIX.[3]

The ASL utterance shown in figure 4.5 does not contain a noun phrase elaborating the trajector of the verb FIX. It is understood that some agent is doing the "fixing," but this agent is not mentioned at all. It is unspecified

3. See chapter 2 for Liddell's (2003) explanation of ASL utterances with nonovert subjects and/or objects where the identity of the agent and/or patient is already salient in the discourse.

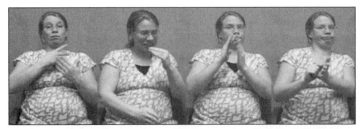

PROJECT   COMPLETE   BOOK   PRINT

FIGURE 4.6. *Three participants' parallel topic-verb structures.*

phonologically and given no grammatical prominence. The ASL utterance, syntactically different from the English passive construction, encodes a construal in which the agent is defocused through both lack of prominence and lack of specificity, analogous to the semantic structure encoded in the passive prompt sentence in English.

Utterances with topic-verb structure were also used in response to another elicitation sentence, shown here as example 2. This prompt consists of two passive clauses, and three of the four of the participants used topic-verb structure to express both clauses.[4]

2. Our project needs to be completed before her new book gets published.

Despite some variation in the determiners, adjectives, adverbs, and repetition of verbs, as shown by translations of the complete utterances

4. Participant D used an English-influenced structure for the second clause, PRO-X BOOK GET PRINT, which was unmarked for topicalization.

in examples 3 through 5, the three utterances are remarkably parallel in their topic-verb structure for both clauses (see figure 4.6, which shows PROJECT, COMPLETE, BOOK, and PRINT as produced by each of the three signers who used topic-verb structure for both clauses).

3. <PRO1.pl.poss PROJECT>topic MUST COMPLETE BEFORE <PRO-X.poss NEW BOOK>topic PRINT

   literal translation: "Our project: must complete before his/her new book: print."

4. <PRO1.pl PROJECT>topic MUST COMPLETE BEFORE <PRO-X NEW BOOK>topic FINISH PRINT, MUST HURRY FINISH

   literal translation: "Our project: must complete before his/her new book: print. [We] have to hurry up and finish [it]."

5. <PRO1.pl PROJECT>topic MUST COMPLETE FINISH #THEN <PRO-X BOOK>topic CAN PRINT

   literal translation: "Our project: must complete; once it's done, his/her book: can print."

As in the previous examples, the topicalized noun phrases are understood to elaborate the landmark of the verb they precede. PROJECT correlates semantically with the landmark of COMPLETE, and BOOK correlates semantically with the landmark of PRINT. None of the six clauses contain overt subjects, and none of the verbs' trajectors are overtly elaborated. With no nominals naming the entities performing either the "completion of the project" or the "publishing," both agents are left completely unspecified and thus defocused in all three utterances.[5]

In all of the examples in this section the signer defocused the agent by not mentioning it overtly. Each of the verbs used in these utterances semantically encodes a relation between an agent (trajector) and a patient (landmark), but there are no overt subjects and no overt objects. The semantic content of the verbs' landmarks correlate with the semantic

5. Some might argue that the identity of the agent of the action MUST COMPLETE is overtly mentioned (albeit in a less specified form) in the pronominal PRO1.pl or PRO1.pl.poss; since the addressee knows that it is "our project," the inference can be made that "we" are the ones who "must complete" it. However, note that the same potential inference does not necessarily hold true for the second clause: just because it is "her book" does not necessarily entail that "she" will be the one carrying out the actual publication. Pronouns that function as possessive determiners cannot be assumed to have agentive referents.

content of nominals produced sentence-initially as topics, so the topicalized nominals are understood as identifying the patient. The verbs' trajectors are not elaborated at all, thus defocusing the agent through both lack of grammatical prominence and lack of phonological specification.

As discussed in chapter 2, the main function of the English passive construction is to defocus the agent through a lack of prominence and lack of specificity. Inherent in the reduction of focus on the agent is a relative increase in the focus on the patient. Because overt subjects are required in English, choosing not to express the agent in subject position necessitates expressing some other entity in that position. In the case of passive, the patient is expressed in subject position. This also provides a relative increase in the focus on the patient.

In the ASL data evoking a defocused agent construal, signers did not express the agent in subject position, but they did not express the patient in subject position, either. Although the meaning is similar, the form of these utterances does not parallel that of the English passive construction. However, perhaps because of the understood increase in prominence for the patient in English passive utterances, patients were predominantly expressed as utterance-initial topicalized nominals, evoking them with a relatively high level of discourse focus while retaining a main-clause utterance in which no overt agent is ever expressed.

Verb-Object Structure

The second most prevalent structure type used to defocus the agent of verbs encoding two-participant events was the verb-object structure.[6] In this structure type, the agent is defocused through a lack of prominence and a lack of specificity, and the patient is expressed in object position.

These utterances parallel the topic-verb structures discussed earlier in that their trajectors are not overtly elaborated; they differ from topic-verb structures in that their landmarks are elaborated as nominals in object position rather than as topics. Whereas the topic-verb utterances evoke a construal with some discourse-level increase in patient focus, verb-object utterances defocus the agent while making no change to the focus on the patient.

These utterances contain two clauses. The initial clause in each example has a verb-object structure and occurs with nonmanual marking, distinguishing it from the following declarative clause. The defocused

6. This structure accounts for 20 percent of the data.

agent construal expressed in the opening clause establishes the generic framework to which the following declarative pertains.

One example of an utterance that begins with a verb-object structure marked as a conditional was produced as a translation of the elicitation sentence: "Rules were made to be broken." The English prompt sentence contains two passive verbs: "were made" and the infinitive "to be broken." The signer produces verbs expressing both of these concepts without nominals elaborating either trajector.

The sentence begins with the clause ESTABLISH RULE, nonmanually marked as a conditional with the eyebrows raised during production of the verb and then lowered during the production of the object (Baker-Shenk and Cokely 1980), thereby creating an "if/when" situation. The semantic structure of the verb ESTABLISH includes both a trajector (the person doing the establishing) and a landmark (the thing established). The nominal RULE follows the verb as direct object, elaborating the landmark of ESTABLISH, but there is no nominal to elaborate the trajector, so the identity of the agent, the person(s) responsible for establishing the rules, is not prominent or specified and is therefore construed as defocused. The defocused agent construal is combined with the conditional "if/when" meaning, resulting in a more generic "whenever" reading.

The following clause contains the auxiliary WILL, followed by an adverbial GUARANTEE and the verb BREAK. The semantics of BREAK include a person doing the breaking (the trajector) and something being broken (the landmark). Neither of these entities is overtly elaborated in the clause; however, the semantic information encoded in the nominal RULE in the previous conditional clause correlates with the semantics of the landmark of BREAK, so the addressee understands that the "rules" are what will be "broken."

The agents of both verbs in the utterance in figure 4.7 are defocused. These gaps in the semantic content are purposely left vague, so that the meaning of the sentence can be understood as a general statement rather than a specific instance with individual agents. As in the English prompt sentence, by leaving the agents unstated, the signer expresses the meaning that whenever rules are established, regardless of who establishes them, they will be broken. This fact is the critical information in the sentence, not the identity of the rule makers or the inevitable rule breakers, whoever they may be.

The utterance in figure 4.8, produced in response to the elicitation sentence "I have never been beaten at chess," is another example in which

< ESTABLISH RULE >cond   WILL GUARANTEE BREAK

FIGURE 4.7. *Utterance with two defocused agent clauses.*

the utterance-initial verb-object clause does not contain a nominal to elaborate its trajector. The use of the conditional marking with a defocused agent clause results in a generic reading similar to that expressed by English impersonal forms such as "when playing chess . . . ."

The second clause in the utterance does include overt expression of its verb's trajector. It consists of a subject pronoun, PRO-1, an adverb, NEVER, and the verb LOSE. The trajector of LOSE is elaborated by the unmarked nominal in subject position, PRO-1. The semantic properties of PRO-1 also correlate with the semantic properties of the trajector of PLAY, and because the declarative clause pertains to the conditional situation established in the preceding clause, PRO-1 can be understood as a specification of the previously unexpressed agent.

The semantic relationships in the sentence shown in figure 4.9 are determined in a similar way. The verb-object clause that begins the sentence, COLLECT R-E-C-E-I-P-T-S, does not contain a nominal elaborating the trajector of COLLECT. The following clause, HAND-TO$^{x \to y}$ SECRETARY TOMORROW, also does not have an overt nominal elaborating the trajector

< PLAY   C-H-E-S-S >cond, PRO-1   NEVER   LOSE
literal translation: "When playing chess, I never lose."

FIGURE 4.8. *Utterance with initial defocused agent expressed in following clause.*

< COLLECT   R-E-C-E-I-P-T-S >cond

MUST   HAND-TO$^{x\rightarrow y}$ SECRETARY   TOMORROW
literal translation: "Once the receipts are collected,
give them to the secretary tomorrow."

FIGURE 4.9. *Utterance with initial defocused agent indicated in the following clause.*

of the verb, but its starting location does indicate a referent to map onto its trajector. Just as in the previous example, it is understood that the same agent is implied for both clauses; the agent in the second clause provides increased specification for the defocused agent of the initial clause.

The verb in the second clause, HAND-TO$^{x\rightarrow y}$, encodes a three-entity event and has a semantic structure similar to that encoded by ditransitive verbs like "give" in English. One of its landmarks is elaborated by the nominal SECRETARY, produced unmarked in object position, and the other landmark correlates semantically with the landmark of the previous clause, R-E-C-E-I-P-T-S.

HAND-TO$^{x\rightarrow y}$ is an indicating verb. In this example it begins with the arm extended toward the addressee in neutral space, indicating the addressee as the referent to map onto the trajector of the verb and giving a reading of the sentence as an imperative statement with second-person "you" as the agent. Because the verb COLLECT does not have an overt nominal elaborating its trajector, the addressee fills in this semantic "blank" with the same agent as the following verb. Thus, the agent, who is understood to be the one "handing" the receipts to the secretary, is also understood to be the one who "collected" those receipts.

In figures 4.8 and 4.9, the trajector of the verb in the initial clause was understood to be semantically correlated with the trajector of the verb in the second clause. At the individual clause level, the verb-object structure provides no grammatical prominence or semantic specification of the trajector, so the agent is defocused. However, some specification and prominence are provided to the initially defocused agent when both clauses are considered together as a conceptual whole. Interactions between prominence and specificity provide composite semantic structures in which the level of focus on the agent is between that of an agent-focused subject-verb-object construction and that of agent-defocused topic-verb structures. The following chapter describes ASL forms that evoke such reduced agent-focused construals.

CONCLUSION

The relative level of focus on an entity in a linguistic utterance is determined by the prominence and specificity with which that entity is expressed. When asked to translate English passive sentences into ASL, the predominant utterance types were structures without overt subjects, in which the trajector is not overtly elaborated and there is no specification of the agent's identity. Through the use of these structures, the ASL translations express a defocused agent construal in terms of both level of prominence (lack of trajector status) and level of specification (not overtly expressed).

In ASL, a defocused agent construal is achieved by not overtly elaborating the trajector; these utterances differ in form from agent-focused utterances only in that they do not include overt subjects. As was previously recognized, ASL sentences without overt subjects are permitted when the identity of the agent is clearly recoverable from context (Liddell 2003; Lucas, Bayley, and Valli 2001). Previous analyses of nonovert-subject sentences have focused on cases in which the agent's identity was previously established in the discourse, either through topicalization or in a previous utterance. The data discussed here show that even when an agent has not previously been overtly expressed, sentences without overt subjects can be used; the resulting utterances evoke a construal in which the agent is defocused.

Leaving the agent unexpressed was the most common strategy that native signers used to produce translations of English passive sentence. Thus it seems from this data set that clauses without overt subjects, known to be used when the agent is already prominent in the discourse (Liddell 2003), can also be readily produced in discourse contexts in which the agent has not previously been identified. Individual ASL utterances that do not include overt elaboration of the trajector encode construals that are analogous to those encoded in passive-voice constructions in English. Additionally, as I explore further in the following chapter, ASL users produce utterances that encode the agent with various levels of agent focus, paralleling the range of English passive and impersonal forms, in which prominence and specificity interact.

Chapter 5

ASL Structures Used to Express Reduced Agent Focus

In addition to fully defocused utterances, which make up the majority of the data elicited as translations of passive sentences from English, some of the ASL utterances express an agent construed as having reduced focus. They do so in one of two ways: the agent is expressed either with overtly elaborated trajectors that occur in underspecified forms and in positions of reduced prominence or through partial elaboration of the trajector, as with indicating verbs and surrogate blends, leading to an interaction between various levels of prominence and specificity. For example, there are ten clauses with indicating verbs and three with surrogate blends in which the trajectors are not overtly elaborated. The combination of the prominence of the agent within the verb and its simultaneous lack of semantic specification results in an overall reduced agent focus. Construals of the agent with reduced focus also occur in the data when the trajector is elaborated overtly, but either expressed in an underspecified form or in a nonprominent position.

The previous chapter described utterances with defocused agent construals associated with syntactic forms in which the trajectors of plain verbs were not overtly elaborated. Signers also produced utterances with reduced focus on the agent, though not complete defocusing. These are shown in the middle light gray section of table 4.2 in chapter 4.

From the discussion in chapter 2 we know that English has a range of impersonalization strategies and that passive constructions fall close to the end of the spectrum with complete agent defocusing. Here we begin to see evidence of a similar range of impersonalization strategies in ASL. In the data, agents are expressed in four different ways that evoke construals with midlevel agent focus: (1) through indicating verbs with unspecified spatial mapping; (2) through constructed action in which the signer blends with a surrogate[1] without overt specification of the surrogate's

---

1. That is, the signer "[takes] on the role" of the agent; see Metzger 1994; Liddell and Metzger 1998; Liddell 2003.

identity; (3) through overt subjects that are semantically underspecified; and (4) through expressing the agent in a syntactically less prominent position (i.e., not in subject position).

In both utterances with indicating verbs and utterances incorporating surrogate blends, the agent is construed with a reduced level of focus: neither fully in focus nor completely defocused but in between. In subjectless utterances with indicating verbs, the agent is unspecified yet somewhat prominent because it is referenced in the conceptually blended signing space. This lack of specificity combined with relative prominence within the verb results in a construal with reduced focus on the agent. Surrogate blends were also used in utterances without overt subjects and with no explicit mention of the event participant that is mapped onto the signer in the blend, as described earlier. These utterances also express reduced focus on the agent, again by leaving the agent's identity unspecified while simultaneously making its role prominent, in this case as the primary actor visible in the blend.

In addition to the unique interactions between specification and prominence brought about by spatial representations used in signed languages, signers also produced utterances with varied levels of grammatical prominence and phonological specificity similar to those seen in spoken languages to express construals with reduced agent focus. These include utterances with overt elaboration of their trajectors as grammatically prominent subjects that are semantically underspecified and utterances with overtly elaborated trajectors in which the agent was semantically and phonologically specified but produced in a grammatical position of reduced prominence.

UNSPECIFIED REFERENTS OF INDICATING VERBS

Some ASL verbs can be meaningfully directed in space. For example, in one group of verbs, the starting and/or ending location of the sign can be directed toward entities to be conceptually mapped onto the trajector and/or the landmark. These are called indicating verbs.[2]

The main focus of previous research on whether ASL utilizes passive constructions has been on indicating verbs (Stokoe, Casterline, and

2. They are also called "agreement verbs" following Padden (1988); the cognitive linguistic framework is used here and follows Liddell's (2000, 2003) definitions and analysis of indicating verbs.

Croneberg 1965; Wilbur 1987; Isenhath 1990; Kegl 1990; Janzen, O'Dea, and Shaffer 2001). Although a search for a passive structure in ASL is not the focus of the current research, the sentence prompts used for this study purposely included concepts that would potentially elicit a variety of ASL verbs, including indicating verbs, and signers did use indicating verbs in ten of the responses to the single-sentence prompts. In response to the sentence in example 1, for instance, all four signers used indicating verbs.

1. Peter wasn't invited to the party.

Though an indicating verb meaning "invite" is used in all four translations, each utterance is structured slightly differently. Two of the signers produced the indicating verb INVITE$^{x \leftarrow y}$, which moves from a location indicating the entity to conceptually map onto its landmark to a location that indicates the entity to map onto its trajector (Liddell 2003; a "backward verb," according to Padden 1988). The other two signers use INVITE$^{\leftarrow y}$, which moves away from the entity to map onto its landmark; the ending location of this sign is in the center of the signing space, a neutral location that does not indicate an entity to map onto the trajector. According to Liddell (2003), although "INVITE$^{\leftarrow y}$ moves to a location ahead of the signer, that movement does not indicate that the signer corresponds to the verb's trajector" (117).

Because the verb INVITE$^{\leftarrow y}$ does not indicate a referent to map onto its trajector, the semantic content of the utterances containing it pattern similarly to utterances with plain verbs. For example, one of the translations using INVITE$^{\leftarrow y}$ is shown in figure 5.1. The signer begins (and ends) her sentence with an interjection expressing a meaning similar to "Unbelievable!" or "I can't believe it!" After the interjection, she fingerspells P-E-T-E-R and indexes a location to her left. She then signs NOT and the verb INVITE$^{\leftarrow y}$. The verb is followed by the prepositional phrase TO PARTY and the final iteration of the interjection.

The indexical sign pointing to the signer's left produced after fingerspelling P-E-T-E-R serves as a conceptual mapping instruction for the addressee. When the verb INVITE$^{\leftarrow y}$ is produced, it begins in a location indicating a space to the signer's left, so through mental space mapping Peter is understood as the person to map onto the landmark of INVITE$^{\leftarrow y}$ as the "invitee." The verb moves just slightly toward a central, neutral location, leaving the trajector of INVITE$^{\leftarrow y}$ not overtly elaborated, so the agent doing the inviting is defocused, just as in the examples with plain verbs in chapter 4.

UNBELIEVABLE   P-E-T-E-R   index^{left}   NOT

INVITE^{←left}   TO   PARTY   UNBELIEVABLE

literal translation: "I can't believe it.
Peter wasn't invited to the party. Unbelievable!"

FIGURE 5.1. *Defocused agent utterance with landmark-only indicating verb.*

The other two signers' translations use the indicating verb INVITE$^{x \leftarrow y}$, in which the ending location of the sign is meaningful and does indicate an entity to map onto the trajector. They do not, however, label the indicated space or provide a nominal that semantically correlates with trajector of INVITE$^{x \leftarrow y}$, thus leaving the identity of the agent underspecified. By moving the sign meaningfully both away from and toward specific locations, the signers indicate both a landmark and a trajector, respectively, but only the landmark is elaborated with an overt nominal. The trajector is prominent enough to be indicated spatially and is partially specified within the phonological structure of the verb, but it is not lexically elaborated. The use of a multivalent verb frames the event as having both an agent and a patient, but the addressee is given no further information about the agent's identity. The agent is reduced in focus; thus the focus of the utterance remains on Peter, the patient.

In the utterance in figure 5.2, the signer indexes a location to her left and then fingerspells P-E-T-E-R, establishing him as the entity to map onto references to that location. Then, with an open hand index, she indexes a location to her right and produces PARTY, providing the mapping

< index^left   P-E-T-E-R >topic   < index^right PARTY >topic

INVITE^{right←left}   NOT

literal translation: "Peter: that party? . . . wasn't invited."

FIGURE 5.2. *Reduced agent focus: trajector indicated but unspecified.*

instructions that link the party with that location. Next the signer uses the indicating verb INVITE,^{x←y} moving it from the space to her left, a location correlated with Peter, to the space to her right, where PARTY was produced. The use of nominals with indexed locations followed by the indicating verb provides the addressee with the mapping instructions to determine that Peter is the (uninvited) "invitee" to a particular event. The addressee can ascertain, from his or her own background knowledge of parties, that someone decided who would and would not be invited to this party. The agent responsible for the inviting, though somewhat prominent through spatial reference in the structure of the indicating verb, is left unspecified and therefore reduced in focus.

The utterance in figure 5.3 also includes the verb INVITE^{x←y}, and the mappings of entities to elaborate its landmark and trajector work similarly, but the structure of the utterance is slightly different and thus warrants further discussion. Here the signer starts with a conditional topic-verb clause, topicalizing the noun PARTY and the verb HOST and producing them slightly forward and to her left in the signing space. The verb HOST encodes an event in which some "host," the trajector, hosts some "event," the landmark. The party is already prominent, and its semantic content

<PARTY>topic   HOST^{forward/left}

P-E-T-E-R^{right}   NOT   INVITE^{forward/left←right}

literal translation: "A party was held. Peter wasn't invited."

FIGURE 5.3. *Utterance with a defocused agent later indicated but unspecified.*

corresponds to the semantic properties of the landmark of HOST, so it is understood that a party was hosted, but because there is no nominal to map onto the trajector of HOST, the agent who hosted the party is both unspecified and nonprominent and therefore defocused.

In the second clause, the signer fingerspells P-E-T-E-R to her right in the signing space, signs NOT, and then produces the indicating verb INVITE^{forward/left←right}, moving it from the location associated with Peter through mental space mappings to the location associated with the hosted party. Note that the signer's nondominant hand remains in the final position of HOST throughout the entire second clause, with the effect that INVITE^{forward/left←right} is clearly moving toward the location where the hosted party was previously (and is still) established.

As in the sentence in figure 5.2, the sentence in figure 5.3 contains no nominal that elaborates the trajector of INVITE. Although the ending location of the sign is meaningful and is understood through the addressee's background knowledge to refer to a person responsible for inviting people to the party, the identity of the party's host is not explicit, and the agent doing the hosting is construed with reduced focus relative to Peter. The sentence is about the fact that Peter was not invited rather than who it was who chose not to invite him.

As in figures 5.1–5.3, with indicating verbs related to "invite," for the verbs GIVE$^{x\rightarrow y}$, GIVE$^{\rightarrow y}$, and HAND-TO$^{x\rightarrow y}$, two of the signers use indicating verbs that meaningfully move to locations, providing mapping instructions for the trajector, while the other two use indicating verbs that do not indicate the entity to map onto the trajector. These utterances differ from the utterances with forms of INVITE, however, in that their verbs are trivalent, encoding three-participant events.

Example 2 is another elicitation sentence that includes the ditransitive English verb "give" as the root verb in a passive construction. The verb "give" encodes an event that involves three entities: an agent (the "giver"), a theme (the "thing being given"), and a goal (in the case of give, the "recipient"). In active constructions in English these are syntactically expressed as subject, direct object, and indirect object, respectively. The ASL sentences produced in response to example 2 used the verbs GIVE$^{x\rightarrow y}$, GIVE$^{\rightarrow y}$, and HAND-TO$^{x\rightarrow y}$, which are indicating verbs that also encode three-entity events.

2. Receipts should be given to the secretary tomorrow.

Figure 5.4 shows an example sentence using GIVE$^{x\rightarrow y}$, and figure 5.5 shows an example sentence using GIVE$^{\rightarrow y}$; the example using HAND-TO$^{x\rightarrow y}$ was shown in figure 4.9. In all three examples, both landmarks are overtly elaborated either as utterance initial nonmanually marked topics or as unmarked nominals in postverbal object position. In figure 5.4 the beginning location of GIVE$^{x\rightarrow y}$ is a position relatively far forward in the signing space, and the signer's facial expression marks the clause as a command. The trajector is indicated but not lexically expressed, leaving the entity to map onto it unspecified; however, the context and facial grammar allow for the indicated trajector to be understood as the addressee. In figure

R-E-C-E-I-P-T-S RECEIPT PLEASE   GIVE$^{x\rightarrow y}$ SECRETARY TOMORROW

FIGURE 5.4. *Reduced agent focus in an utterance expressing a trivalent event.*

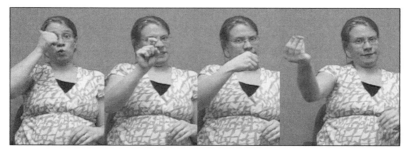

TOMORROW   MUST   GIVE^{→y}

RECEIPTS   TO-index   SECRETARY

FIGURE 5.5. *Defocused agent utterance expressing a trivalent event.*

5.5, the indicating verb GIVE^{→y} is used, beginning in a neutral position and indicating only a landmark and leaving the trajector unindicated, unspecified, and defocused.

In ASL, utterances with verbs that indicate trajectors that are not overtly specified are similar to those described by Janzen, O'Dea, and Shaffer (2001) as instances of ASL passive constructions. There is reduced focus on the agent, and, "rather than specifying an agent in the syntax by associating an agent NP with a particular locus, the locus is empty. . . . the movement of the agreement verb begins at a morphosyntactic, but semantically empty, locus" (289–90).[3] However, the examples given here differ from Janzen et al.'s definition of prototypical passive in one critical way: the events are not viewed from the patient's perspective. The signers present the information from the narrator's perspective, which is not identified with either the agent or the patient.

Only two utterances in the data were presented from the patient's perspective. They were both given in response to the English prompt

3. The descriptions used in this book follow Liddell's (2003) analysis of indicating verbs rather than agreement verbs, so I do not use the term *locus*, but the structures described are the same.

NO-ONE BEAT$^{X \rightarrow 1}$ PRO-1

A-T C-H-E-S-S NONE EVER-SINCE

literal translation: "No one has beaten me at chess. Nobody. Ever."

FIGURE 5.6. *Utterance with underspecified subject and patient perspective.*

sentence in example 3. One of them, shown in figure 5.6, includes an overt nominal, the impersonal pronoun NO-ONE as the overt subject elaborating the trajector of BEAT$^{X \rightarrow 1}$, and is thus an example of reduced focus on the agent through the use of an impersonal pronoun in an active sentence with patient perspective rather than what Janzen et al. would label a passive construction. The other, shown in figure 5.7, qualifies as a "prototypical passive" following Janzen et al.'s definitions. It contains an indicating verb that is meaningfully directed in space to indicate entities to map onto both trajector and landmark, but there is no overt noun phrase to elaborate its trajector, so its beginning location is semantically unspecified; the agent is defocused and not mentioned. The signer is understood to represent the patient through mental space mapping, and the event is presented from the patient's perspective.

3.   I have never been beaten at chess.

This is the only instance of this type of utterance that occurs anywhere in my data. Even though this structure is arguably a prototypical passive construction because of its syntactic structure, the use of a passive construction is evidently not the typical way that ASL signers express defocused or reduced focus agents.

< PRO-1	PLAY	CHESS >cond

PRO-1	NEVER	BEAT$^{X \to 1}$	NEVER

literal translation: "When I play chess, I'm never beaten. Never."

FIGURE 5.7. *Utterance with indicated but unspecified subject and patient perspective.*

This section has shown how the dimensions of prominence and specificity interact in unique ways in the ASL data when the identity of referents is mapped onto the signing space. Indicating verbs are used even when the entity to map onto the space indicated is not overtly elaborated. In these instances the trajector is prominent enough to be indicated spatially but is not as prominent as an overt nominal; the identity of the trajector is unspecified even though its location is mapped in the signing space. Thus, focus on the agent is reduced relative to an overtly specified transitive clause but not defocused to the same extent as in an utterance with no overt elaboration of the trajector.

UNSPECIFIED SURROGATES IN CONCEPTUAL BLENDS

Another way that the participants evoked a construal in which the agent received midlevel focus was to use surrogate blends to depict the actions of unspecified agents. The data include surrogate blends that visibly depict the actions of agents even when the identity of those agents is

RECOMMEND^{→up}   TURN-DOWN

PRESIDENT   TURN-DOWN

FIGURE 5.8. *Utterance with unspecified surrogate blend:* RECOMMEND.

not overtly specified. The agent is highly prominent due to its visibility in the blend, but the lack of specificity leaves the referent generic, resulting in reduced focus on the identity of the agent and increased focus on the action being performed. The semantic content of the prompt sentences provided only limited opportunities to use surrogate blends, so only three utterances using unspecified surrogate blends are found in the data set.[4]

Two of the three unspecified surrogate blends occurred as the initial clause in translations of another elicitation sentence: "The recommendation was vetoed by the president." In both cases, the verb RECOMMEND is produced in a clause without an overtly elaborated trajector. The form of RECOMMEND is a schematic iconic representation of a person presenting something to someone in a position of authority, represented by the movement toward a higher position within the signing space. In figure 5.8, the signer's gaze shifts away from the addressee during production of

4. The prompts designed to elicit narrative structures provided more opportunities for signers to shift between depicted characters and construct the action from a variety of perspectives; the narrative data contain many more examples of the constructed action of unspecified agents depicted in surrogate blends.

PRO-X.POSS   BICYCLE   NOW   #F-I-X   depict: fix

FIGURE 5.9. *Utterance with unspecified surrogate blend: FIX.*

RECOMMEND and toward the conceptualized location of the entity understood as the "intended receiver of the recommendation." The signer's
face simultaneously depicts an anxious or hopeful expression understood
to represent the emotions of the person making the recommendation. She
is prominently depicting the agent's actions through the surrogate blend,
but the agent's identity has no semantic specification. This combination
of prominence without specificity evokes a construal of the agent with
reduced focus; the clause is about the fact that a recommendation was
made rather than about the person who made it.

The third utterance in which an agentive surrogate was left unspecified
was produced in response to the following elicitation sentence: "His bike
is being repaired." This response consists of a topic-verb structure (discussed in chapter 4) followed by a second clause that consists only of the
verb depicting the unspecified agent's action.

As in the utterance in figure 5.8, the signer's gaze during the depiction
of "fix" in figure 5.9 is directed away from the addressee. In this case the
signer has blended with a surrogate representing the person doing the fixing, and her gaze is directed toward the conceptualized object she is fixing.
She is understood to be representing the agent's actions, but the agent's
identity is not specified. The action used to depict the act of fixing is also
semantically underspecified. She alternates her hands back and forth and
simultaneously wiggles her fingers as if manipulating small objects. This
is a schematic iconic representation of the event rather than a specified
role-play of the actual motions involved in repairing a bicycle.

Indicated locations in signing space conceptualized as referents to map
onto trajector and landmark, eye gaze away from the addressee and toward a conceptualized entity, and facial expression corresponding to that
of the understood agent all serve as markers of these clauses as depictive
of the agent's action. The agent is visible in the blend and depicted at a

Reduced Agent Focus : 67

life-size scale, both of which serve to increase the agent's prominence. The event is also represented from agent's perspective, making the agent even more prominent. Despite all of this prominence, the trajector is not lexically elaborated, leaving the agent's identity unspecified. Here again, as with indicating verbs, both prominence and specificity influence the level of focus, and their interaction leads to a construal of the agent with reduced focus as opposed to completely defocused.

UNDERSPECIFICATION OF SUBJECTS

In the elicited ASL translations of passive sentences in English, twenty-four multivalent verb tokens occur in clauses with overt nominals elaborating their trajectors. However, even with overtly elaborated trajectors, fully half of these utterances are produced in ways that limit the agent's construed level of focus. These overtly elaborated trajectors are reduced in focus in two ways: the overt expression of the agent occurs either in a form with reduced specificity, as described here, or in a position of reduced prominence, as described in the following section.

Six of the elicited utterances have subjects that are semantically underspecified, reducing the relative level of focus on the agent. Several different impersonalization strategies are used in this data set to achieve underspecification: (1) use of indefinite pronouns, (2) a plural noun with generic reference, (3) pronouns with unspecified referents, and (4) a metonymic use of an inanimate entity as the agent. Let us consider each of these strategies in turn.

Indefinite pronouns were used as the subject in two of the elicited utterances produced in subject-verb-object constructions. An example of this is shown in figure 5.10, which was produced in response to the following elicitation sentence: "I have never been beaten at chess." The nominal NO-ONE is expressed in subject position, making it highly prominent, but it does not fully specify the agent's identity.

The other instance in which an indefinite pronoun is used occurs in an utterance with topic-subject-verb structure produced in response to the following elicitation sentence: "That old car will never be stolen." The utterance, shown in figure 5.11, includes the topic THAT OLD #CAR, which elaborates the landmark of STEAL, and the indefinite pronoun NO-ONE as an unmarked nominal overtly elaborating the trajector of STEAL, in subject position. The level of focus on the agent is reduced by using the

NO-ONE BEAT$^{X \to 1}$ PRO-1

A-T C-H-E-S-S NONE EVER-SINCE

literal translation: "No one has beaten me at chess. Nobody. Ever."

FIGURE 5.10. *Agent expressed as indefinite pronoun:* NO-ONE.

< THAT OLD #CAR >topic

NO-ONE WILL STEAL*

literal translation: "That old car? No one will steal . . . ."

FIGURE 5.11. *Assumed agent expressed as indefinite pronoun:* NO-ONE.

*THAT is directed toward the signer's right, indicating that she will represent the location of the OLD #CAR in that part of her signing space. STEAL is located in signing space at same location that was established to represent the car.

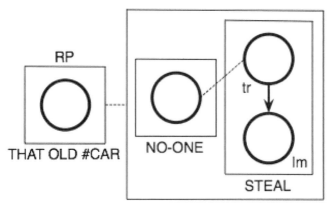

FIGURE 5.12. *Diagram of the utterance in figure 5.11.*

underspecified indefinite pronoun NO-ONE despite its prominent grammatical position. The agent is not left unexpressed, so it is not defocused to the extent of the construal invoked by the English prompt sentence, but it is reduced relative to an utterance with a fully specified, grounded nominal elaborating the trajector. The semantic structure of the utterance in figure 5.11 is represented in figure 5.12.

For the same prompt sentence, "That old car will never be stolen," one signer produced a translation with PEOPLE as the overt subject (figure 5.13). Although the subject is a nominal, two underspecification strategies (Langacker 2006) are invoked through the use of this noun. First, the semantic content of PEOPLE is highly schematic, providing only a broad characterization; second, it encodes a plural referent, which is inherently less delimited than the referent of a singular noun. Both of these factors make it more difficult for the addressee to conceptualize a specific agent. Although the agent is overtly expressed with a nominal in subject position, the fact that this nominal encodes an underspecified (schematic and plural) referent results in a construal in which the focus on the agent is reduced.

Two utterances include pronouns as the overt subject, which clearly reference locations in space to map onto them, but the referenced locations have not been identified, leaving these pronouns semantically unspecified. Both utterances containing underspecified pronouns were produced as translations of example 4, with the underspecified pronouns elaborating the trajector of RECOMMEND, which is expressed as an impersonal nominalization in the English prompt.

4. The recommendation was vetoed by the president.

< #CAR   index   OLD >topic

< PEOPLE STEAL >rh FINEwig WONT PSHAW

FIGURE 5.13. *Utterance with agent expressed as schematic plural:* PEOPLE.

In figure 5.14, the overt subject is a personal pronoun that indicates a location within the signing space to conceptually map onto the verb's trajector. However, this pronoun does not have an antecedent, and no entity has previously been established in that location, so the result is a

< index$^{\rightarrow X}$ RECOMMEND$^{X \rightarrow up}$ >top

PRESIDENT   TURN-DOWN

FIGURE 5.14. *Utterance with a pronominal subject with unspecified referent.*

< index^{→area}   RECOMMEND^{→up} >topic

PRESIDENT   TURN-DOWN

FIGURE 5.15. *Utterance with unspecified spatial reference in subject position.*

semantically empty pronoun. The lack of specification reduces the level of focus on the agent.

In figure 5.15 the pronoun used is a generic form. It is phonologically produced with a relaxed 5 handshape, which moves in a small arc with the palm facing downward. The pronoun indicates a general area of the signing space to conceptually map onto its referent. The pronoun is similar to the one in figure 5.14 in that it is used without previous mention of any entities to serve as antecedent. Additionally, the arc movement indicates plural referents, and because the area is only roughly specified, the entities it refers to are construed in a vague sense. These three strategies—lack of an overt antecedent, plurality, and underspecification—all reduce the focus on the agent, and the combination of all three results in a form used as a generic reference pronoun.

The final utterance with an underspecified overt subject was produced in response to the following elicitation sentence "The results will be published in the newspaper tomorrow" (figure 5.16). The nominal NEWSPAPER is an inanimate entity expressed as the subject, thereby construing it as agentive through metonymy. It is understood to refer to the "people who produce the newspaper," which is a plural underspecified agent for the verb PRINT. Both the plural form and the additional abstraction away

TODAY   RESULT   TOMORROW NEWSPAPER WILL   PRINT

FIGURE 5.16. *Utterance with inanimate subject.*

from the agent through metonymy serve to reduce the salience of the agent in the utterance; thus the construal can be analyzed as impersonal.

Although the trajectors of the verbs in these utterances are elaborated overtly and in grammatically prominent subject position, their agents are construed with reduced focus because they are expressed using underspecified forms rather than fully specified nominals. They therefore semantically parallel impersonal forms in English.

REDUCED PROMINENCE THROUGH WORD ORDER

In six of the responses to individual English passive sentences, a rhetorical question construction was used in the ASL translation.[5] In these utterances a topicalized noun phrase is produced initially and is followed immediately by the verb and then a rhetorical question; the answer to the rhetorical question, the nominal elaborating the verb's trajector, is expressed as the final phrase in the utterance.

Two of the signers produced sentences with rhetorical question-answer sequences in response to the sentence in example 5, which includes an overt *by*-phrase naming the agent. For example, the utterance shown in figure 5.17 begins with the signer's head tilted backward, signaling a rhetorical question. This nonmanual marker continues through the first four signs: TONIGHT FOOD MAKE WHO. While her head is tilted back to mark the rhetorical question, the signer also raises her eyebrows to mark the temporal adverb TONIGHT and the noun FOOD as a topic. During the verb MAKE, the signer's eyebrows are in neutral position;

5. Wilbur (1994) argues that the correct analysis of these structures is as pseudoclefts. Though I agree with her analysis, and the arguments here support her description of the function of these structures, for clarity, I have kept the more widely used label rhetorical questions.

<< TONIGHT   FOOD >topic   MAKE   <WHO>whq >rhq

S-A-L-L-Y   MAKE++
literal translation: "Tonight's dinner: made by who?
Sally. [She'll] make [it]."

FIGURE 5.17. *Utterance with agent expressed as an answer to a rhetorical question.*

as she produces WHO, her eyebrows are lowered and brought together, marking a *wh*-question. Once the question sign has been produced, the signer's face returns to a neutral, unmarked position as she answers the rhetorical question by fingerspelling S-A-L-L-Y.

    5.   Dinner is going to be made by Sally tonight.

    Utterances with rhetorical question structure consist of multiple clauses, and the level of focus on the agent differs in each clause. In figure 5.17 the nominal S-A-L-L-Y is not produced in the first clause with the verb MAKE. It is expressed toward the end of the utterance in a separate clause. The agent's identity is initially unspecified and grammatically reduced in prominence. The dinner and its production are expressed without an agent, directing the addressee's attention to the event. In the final clause, however, the focus shifts to the agent. The trajector is overtly elaborated in subject position, expressing the agent's identity in a fully specified and prominent way. The verb of the final clause is again MAKE, allowing the addressee to understand Sally as the agent of the previous utterance as well. The agent is defocused in the main clause and focused in the second

<RULE>topic <MAKE WHAT-FOR-FOR>rhq BREAK RULE THAT TEND
literal translation: "Rules? . . . made for? To break, typically."

FIGURE 5.18. *Utterance with three defocused agents: topic-verb-rhetorical, verb-object, and verb structure.*

clause. Utterances in which the agent is expressed as the answer to a rhetorical question can therefore be used to effectively shift the discourse focus from a nonagent entity to the agent, with the final result of directing the addressee's attention to the agent (as argued by Wilbur 1994).

Here is one final example of a structure containing a rhetorical question: in one response to the sentence in example 6, the signer produces a topic-verb-rhetorical structure and answers the rhetorical question using a clause with a verb-object structure. The noun phrase that elaborates the landmark of the verb MAKE is the first sign, RULE, which is nonmanually marked as a topic. The next signs, MAKE and #WHAT-FOR-FOR co-occur with nonmanual signals for a rhetorical question: the head is tilted backward and shakes slightly, the eyebrows are raised, and the eye gaze is directed away from the addressee. Then, in answer to her rhetorical question, the signer produces a clause with a verb-object structure. Finally, she adds another clause, marked with a lowered head and lowered eye gaze, which consists of a discourse marker and a verb.

6. Rules were made to be broken.

Consider each verb separately. The verb MAKE is produced as part of a rhetorical question. Its landmark is elaborated by the noun RULE, which is topicalized. Its trajector is not elaborated. There is no unmarked noun phrase in the clause that contains MAKE. It has neither an overt subject nor an overt object. It is an instance of the topic-verb-rhetorical structure, and its agent is unspecified. The next verb is BREAK. An overt object, the unmarked noun RULE, immediately follows this verb. The trajector of BREAK is not elaborated; there is no overt noun phrase before this verb within this clause. This is a token of the verb-object structure. The final clause contains only a discourse marker and the verb TEND, preceded only by a discourse marker; it has no overt arguments at all. The discourse marker THAT in this context may be analyzed as a discourse-level topic, referencing the semantic content of the utterance preceding it; the meaning would be something akin to "Breaking rules? That's what tends to happen." Note that the trajector is not overtly elaborated in any of the three clauses in the ASL sentence, and thus the meaning conveyed does not include a specified agent for any of these actions; the signer does not tell us who is "making" the rules, who is "breaking" them, or who "tends" to do such things.

CONCLUSION

The ASL utterances with the least focus on the agent are those with both reduced prominence and a lack of specificity; these constructions are semantically equivalent to, though syntactically distinct from, the English passive construction. Although ASL may have a syntactically passive construction (as previous research on agreement verbs suggests; see Janzen, O'Dea, and Shaffer 2001), based on the data analyzed here, it is not the primary strategy used to express defocused agent construal.

In addition to differences in focus level based on whether there is an overt lexical elaboration of the trajector, the focus on the agent in an ASL utterance also varies with the amount of information the verb expresses about the agent. In ASL, verbs can be categorized with respect to the amount of information they provide about the involved participants: plain verbs do not identify their participants within their phonological form; indicating verbs reference the location of a conceived entity in the signing space; and depicting verbs produced in surrogate blends represent their participants visually as the signer constructs their actions. All of these types of verbs can be used in clauses without overt nominals elaborating their trajectors; the resulting interactions between prominence and specificity evoke construals with reduced focus on the agent. This range of construals is semantically analogous to those evoked by English impersonal forms.

Chapter 6

Agent Focus in ASL Texts

When multiple utterances are combined into a text, the level of focus on a given entity is determined by its semantic specificity and grammatical prominence at two levels: within each individual utterance and within the structure of the discourse unit when viewed as a whole. At the utterance level (see chapters 4 and 5), the specificity of the semantic content interacts with grammatical prominence to create a particular construal. At the discourse level, as this chapter explains, each utterance builds upon the conceptualization established by preceding utterances, increasing or reducing focus on entities previously established, as well as potentially introducing new entities.

To get a sense of how this works, consider the text in example 1, which is one of the text elicitation prompts. The first sentence introduces the domain of scientific experimentation, which serves as the context for the following utterances. The second sentence focuses on the volunteers, explicitly naming them in subject position, fully specified and highly prominent. Noun phrases and pronouns referring to the volunteers (*them, they, the others, the people*) elaborate the trajector of each verb in the rest of the text, maintaining and reinforcing a construal in which the volunteers are the most salient entity. Simultaneously and conversely, the agent performing the experiments is never overtly mentioned. The use of passive constructions without *by*-phrases allows for the continued non-agent-focused construal throughout the text.

1. **English Prompt Text: Scientific Experiment on REM Sleep**
   Experiments show that REM sleep definitely can help you learn better. In one test, volunteers **were taught** a new skill. That night, some of them **were awakened** whenever they entered REM sleep. The others **were awakened** the same number of times, but only during non-REM sleep. The next day, the people who got their REM sleep tested better than the others at *performing* the new skill.

When asked to translate this text (and the three other prompt texts), the participants produced translations with an analogous conceptual structure, using utterances without overt subjects and leaving the identity of the agents unstated. This chapter describes their linguistic choices and considers how the level of agent focus in each clause affects the construal of agents in the text as a whole.

Because the level of focus is affected by the relationship between prominence and specificity, the agent's syntactic position and semantic content must both be determined. The approach used in analyzing whether and how agents are defocused in the elicited ASL texts incorporates both semantic and syntactic aspects, reflecting the depth of the symbolic relationship between form and meaning. The initial semantic approach involves determining how many agents are included in the text and the identity of each one. Once the agents have been identified, the texts are analyzed to determine whether each agent is overtly expressed. Agents that are never expressed overtly are not in focus in the text. Those that are defocused in a particular clause can be expressed as a focused entity either earlier or later in the narrative, thereby affecting the overall construal of that entity evoked by the text as a whole.

In order to begin to study the ways that defocused agents are expressed and understood at the discourse level in ASL, ASL data were elicited through translations of English texts. This English-to-ASL text translation task was designed to provide an agent-defocused construal to see how ASL users would express it. The analysis of the resulting ASL narratives shows that they used both defocused and reduced focus agent forms in particular ways and at particular points in their narratives to evoke overall construals analogous to those in the English prompts.

Each of the following four sections begins with a discussion of an English prompt text; once we have an understanding of the semantic agents in the English text and their encoding, we will be in a good position to make a parallel analysis of an elicited ASL translation, which allows direct comparisons of the linguistic strategies for defocusing agents in the two languages. That analysis proceeds in the same way as the English analysis: the semantic content of each text is considered, particularly with regard to the identity of the agents. This is followed by a discussion of the syntactic structures and phonological forms used when the agents are defocused. For each prompt text, one representative translation guides the discussion.

ASL TEXT DATA: PALEONTOLOGY

The first text, given in example 2, describes the work of paleontologists. Table 6.1 lists each verb in the English text, along with the root

TABLE 6.1. *Verbs in English Text Prompt: Dinosaurs*

Token	Valence	Construction Type	Elaboration of Trajector	Identity of Agent
know	divalent	active	as the subject - non-specific	we - generic pronoun
are being discovered	**divalent**	**passive**	**not overtly elaborated**	*someone*
study	divalent	active	as the subject - relative clause	scientists
learn	divalent	infinitive	earlier in the discourse	scientists
have	divalent	active	as the subject	paleontologists
keeping up with	divalent	gerund	earlier in the discourse	paleontologists
are discovered	**divalent**	**passive**	**not overtly elaborated**	*someone*
is	monovalent	stative	as the subject	it - dummy subject
know	**divalent**	**infinitive**	**not overtly elaborated**	*people*
belong to	divalent	active	as the subject	they - bones
is	monovalent	stative	as the subject	it - animal
know	monovalent	active	as the subject - non-specific	we - generic pronoun
are	monovalent	stative	as the subject	bones
must be	monovalent	modal	as the subject	scientists
separate	divalent	infinitive	earlier in the discourse	scientists
identify	divalent	infinitive	earlier in the discourse	scientists

verb's valence in the second column and the construction type with which it is expressed in the third column. The fourth column indicates whether the trajector of each verb is overtly elaborated, and, if so, where in the discourse that elaboration occurs.[1] The fifth column gives the identity of the agent in the event encoded by each verb; implicit agents (i.e., the understood or assumed identity of trajectors that are not explicitly elaborated) are given in italics. The bold rows mark verbs for which the agent is construed as defocused or with reduced focus; the trajectors of those verbs are not overtly elaborated anywhere in the narrative.

2. **English Text Prompt: Dinosaurs**

Today we know of more than a thousand species of dinosaurs, and others **are being discovered** every year. Paleontologists, scientists who study bones and fossils to learn about the past, have a tough job keeping up with all the bones. When bones **are first discovered**, it is sometimes difficult to know what animal they belong to. Is it a new dinosaur or one we already know about? And when the bones of more than one creature are jumbled together, scientists must be careful to separate and identify each animal.

As shown in table 6.1, five of the sixteen verbs in the English prompt text have trajectors that are not specifically elaborated. The verb *discover* is used twice in passive constructions without *by*-phrases. The identity of the agent in both instances is not overtly specified in the text; this evokes a construal in which the identity of the person who is making the initial discoveries is not directly relevant to the text, placing the focus on the act of discovery and the scientific work of analysis and identification. The verb *know* occurs three times, twice as an active verb with a generic reference pronoun as its subject and once as an infinitive without an overtly elaborated trajector. The analysis of the ASL translations is centered around how ASL signers convey the meaning expressed by these five English verbs.

A glossed transcription of one signer's translation is given in example 3.

---

1. Note that with impersonalized forms such as gerunds and infinitives, the immediate clause does not include overt elaboration of the trajector. However, in some cases the identity of the agent can be recovered by the addressee from previous discourse. In other cases, the trajector is not overtly elaborated either in the immediate clause or elsewhere in the discourse, evoking a defocused agent construal.

3. Gloss of Participant A's translation of the paleontology text

      <DINOSAUR>top TODAY **HAVE** FINISH **IDENTIFY**++ ONE-
THOUSAND DIFFERENT++ S-P-E-C-I-E-S #OF DINOSAUR
EVERY-YEAR MORE+ **FIND**++ / index <SCIENTIST WHO
SPECIALTY B-O-N-E / STUDY$^{\rightarrow|fossils|}$ F-O-S-S-I-L STUDY$^{\rightarrow|fossils|}$
LEARN ABOUT LONG-AGO HISTORY LOOK-OVER$^{\rightarrow|fossils|}$
/ index$^{\rightarrow|scientist|}$>rh **NAME** P-A-L-E-O-N-T-O-L-O-G-I-S-T
PRO$^{\rightarrow|scientist|}$ HARD TIME FOLLOW++ PICK-UP NEW++

      FIRST FIND WELL MUST FIGURE-OUT / OH-I-SEE /
<WHICH ANIMAL / PRO.poss$^{[multiple]\rightarrow|animals|}$>whq

      <NEW++>q #OR SAME FINISH+ **NOTICE** PAST / LOOK-
OVER$^{\rightarrow|fossils|}$

      <IF DIFFERENT+ ANIMAL **MIX**++>cond WELL SCIENTIST MUST-
#BE CAREFUL+ SEPARATE+ PRO.poss$^{[multiple]\rightarrow|animals|}$ WOW-SHAKE

The verbs used in the ASL text in (3) are listed in table 6.2. The layout of the table is the same as in table 6.1 above. The rows in bold in the table mark the verbs that encode two-participant events with animate agents that are not overtly expressed.

Just as in the English text, the ASL translation begins with clauses that do not have overtly specified agents in order to keep the focus on the dinosaurs and their discovery. No overt nominals appear before the verbs HAVE, IDENTIFY, and FIND to elaborate their trajectors.

As discussed in chapter 4, the ASL verb HAVE often occurs without an overt subject and with no identifiable agent recoverable from the previous context. In these subjectless constructions, HAVE can be said to function as an existential, informing the addressee of the state of events rather than establishing a possessive relationship. The semantic properties of ASL clauses in which HAVE is used without an overt subject and with no previously stated agent parallel those of the English "there is" existential construction.

The other two verbs in the opening section of the narrative that do not have overtly elaborated trajectors are IDENTIFY and FIND. The unspecified agent of IDENTIFY can be determined only after the word S-P-E-C-I-E-S provides the needed clue that the narrative is scientific in nature, allowing the addressee to fill in the implicit agent from background knowledge and context. The verb FIND is also understood to be elaborated by the same unspecified agent. Both of these verbs are produced in neutral space in front of the signer as plain verbs with

TABLE 6.2. *Verbs Used in ASL Translation of English Text on Paleontology: Participant A*

Token	Valence	Verb Type	Elaboration of Trajector	Identity of Agent
HAVE	divalent	plain	not overtly elaborated	n/a - existential
IDENTIFY++	divalent	plain	not overtly elaborated	*scientist*
FIND++	divalent	plain	not overtly elaborated	*someone*
STUDY	divalent	surrogate blend	as the subject	SCIENTIST
STUDY	divalent	surrogate blend	earlier in the discourse	SCIENTIST
LEARN	divalent	surrogate blend	earlier in the discourse	SCIENTIST
LOOK-AT++	divalent	surrogate blend	earlier in the discourse	SCIENTIST
NAME	divalent	plain	not overtly elaborated	*people*
FOLLOW++	divalent	surrogate blend	as the subject	PRO3 - paleontologist
PICK-UP	divalent	surrogate blend	earlier in the discourse	PRO3 - paleontologist
FIND	divalent	plain	not overtly elaborated	*someone*
MUST	divalent	modal	not overtly elaborated	*paleontologist*
FIGURE-OUT	divalent	plain	not overtly elaborated	*paleontologist*
NOTICE	divalent	plain	not overtly elaborated	*scientists*
LOOK-AT+	divalent	surrogate blend	earlier in the discourse	PRO3 - paleontologist
MIX++	divalent	plain	not overtly elaborated	n/a - stative
SEPARATE+	divalent	surrogate blend	earlier in the discourse	SCIENTIST

IDENTIFY   FIND

FIGURE 6.1. *Plain verbs used with defocused agents.*

reduplication marking the plurality of their landmarks, while the signer's gaze is directed at the addressee (figure 6.1).

Once the topic of the text has been established, the ASL narrative structure continues to parallel the English text, using a subject/relative clause/verb structure with multiple clauses embedded in the relative clause, and overtly establishing SCIENTIST as the subject. Once SCIENTIST has been introduced as a subject, it becomes the most prominent agentive entity in the narrative and therefore serves to elaborate the trajector of each of the following divalent verbs (following Liddell 2003). The pronominal with "paleontologist" as its antecedent is the next prominent entity and thus also elaborates the trajector of several verbs in a row that do not have overt subjects.

Here the interaction between clause- and discourse-level agent focus can be seen. Subjectless clauses are used in some cases in which the identity of the agent can be recovered by the addressee from previous discourse. In these situations, although the agent lacks prominence and specificity within the clause itself because the trajector is in fact overtly elaborated at a discourse level, the resulting overall structure does not evoke a defocused agent construal. When the trajector is not overtly elaborated either in the immediate clause or elsewhere in the discourse, the resulting construal does have a defocused agent.

The next sentence in the English text, which begins as shown in example 4a, contains three verbs: a passive construction in the opening adverbial clause, a stative verb with a dummy *it* as the subject of the main clause, and an infinitive. The ASL translation, for which the glossed transcription is given in example 4b, includes the verbs FIND and MUST FIGURE-OUT without overt subjects. The signer produces these signs in a neutral position in the center of her signing space while facing forward

| FIRST | FIND | MUST | FIGURE-OUT |

FIGURE 6.2. *The verbs* FIND *and* MUST FIGURE-OUT *without overt subjects.*

(see figure 6.2). The addressee is responsible for determining the identity of the intended agents through context.

4a. When bones are first discovered, it is sometimes difficult to know . . .

4b. FIRST FIND WELL MUST FIGURE-OUT . . .

This signer uses the verb NOTICE for her translation of the final clause from the English text that has an unspecified agent: *or one we already know about.* Just as in the English text, this signer produces the utterance (figure 6.3) as part of a comparison. She begins with NEW marked as a yes/no question and shifted to her left with her chin lowered. She then signs #OR while shifting to the right side of the signing space. The following clause is produced on the right side with the signer's head tilted back and leaning to the side, contrasting it with <NEW++>q. The verb NOTICE occurs in this back/right position with no overt nominal elaborating its trajector. At the end of the utterance, the signer shifts forward and directs her gaze downward and to the left, evidence that she is producing a surrogate blend. This is the same body position she used earlier for LEARN$^{\rightarrow|\text{fossils}|}$ and STUDY$^{\rightarrow|\text{fossils}|}$ (figure 6.4), for which the SCIENTIST overtly elaborated the trajector, so the agent of LOOK-OVER$^{\rightarrow|\text{fossils}|}$ at the end of the utterance illustrated in figure 6.3 is understood to be the same representative "scientist" as previously established in the discourse.

Two other verbs in the ASL narrative do not have previously established overt agents: MIX and NAME. The verb MIX occurs in a subject-verb utterance with a subject, ANIMAL, which is semantically inconsistent with the agent. Similar to the examples discussed in chapter 4, the form of MIX is ambiguous: it could be analyzed as a divalent verb or a predicate adjective. In this instance (figure 6.5), it is construed as a stative description rather than an event and is thus analyzed as a predicate adjective.

<NEW++>q　　　　　#OR　　　　　SAME

FINISH+　　　　　NOTICE　　　　　PAST

/ LOOK-OVER→|fossils|

FIGURE 6.3. *Utterance containing* NOTICE *used without a specified agent.*

FIGURE 6.4. *Signer as* |scientist|.

<IF　　　DIFFERENT　　　ANIMAL　　　MIX++>cond

FIGURE 6.5. *Conditional clause with* MIX *as a predicate adjective.*

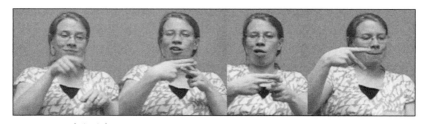

index$^{\rightarrow|\text{scientist}|}$>top   NAME   fs:P-(aleontologist)

FIGURE 6.6. *Utterance containing* NAME, *used without a specified agent.*

Interestingly, the clause in figure 6.5 was expressed as a translation of the English utterance *when the bones of more than one creature are jumbled together,* in which the form *are jumbled* is also ambiguous between these two readings and construed as a stative description.

The ASL verb NAME$^{\rightarrow y}$ can also be construed as either encoding an event or describing a state. Like its English semantic counterpart, "be called," NAME$^{\rightarrow y}$ is used much more often to tell the addressee the name of a particular entity than to express a situation in which the entity was given its name. When used without an overt elaboration of its trajector and with the intention of simply providing the appropriate label for an entity, it is construed as encoding a stative relationship between the entity and its name rather than as an event. Because NAME$^{\rightarrow y}$ is rarely used with an overt subject, it is often glossed as BE-CALLED (Klima and Bellugi 1979) or NAMED (Janzen, O'Dea, and Shaffer 2001). However, there is nothing in the phonological form of this verb that marks it as passive, so the use of an English participle or passive form in the gloss is potentially misleading. It is simply a verb with a defocused agent serving to encode a stative relationship (see figure 6.6).

All four signers used similar structures to evoke defocused agent construals in their translations of the English text. For the opening sentences, they all used either HAVE or FIND or both in subjectless clauses and without overtly elaborated trajectors. For the second passive verb, "are discovered," two of the other signers also used FIND without an explicit

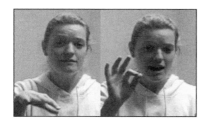

FIGURE 6.7. *Examples of* FIND *in surrogate blends.*

agent (figure 6.1), but they produced it in a surrogate blend with eye gaze away from the addressee (figure 6.7).

Where Participant A defocused the agent of NOTICE, Participant C used a similar syntactic structure with FIND. At the end of the narrative, all four signers used constructed action with unspecified surrogate blends to depict the actions of a generic paleontologist attempting to determine which bones belong to which animals.

ASL TEXT DATA: ELIZABETH SMART

The semantic structure of the second text, given in example 5, differs from the prompt text about paleontologists. Rather than having a few unspecified, generic entities who continue to be the agents throughout the text (as we saw with *scientist*), in this case each of the verbs without an overt elaboration of its trajector refers to a different agent.

5. **English Text Prompt: Elizabeth Smart**
   "Elizabeth Smart **Found** Alive"

   Salt Lake City, Utah (CNN)—Missing teenager Elizabeth Smart, the subject of an intense police *hunt* since she **was reported** *abducted* from her bedroom last summer, **was found** alive Wednesday and **reunited** with her family . . .

   Police **were tipped** to the suspect's whereabouts by two callers who had seen his photograph and knew he **was wanted** for *questioning* in Elizabeth's disappearance.

The first sentence of the text includes four defocused agent forms: "was reported," "abducted," "was found," and "[was] reunited." The implicit agent in each case is different; the people hunting for her were not the same people who reported her missing, nor were they the ones who abducted her, eventually found her, or reunited her with her family. We know from the text that the police are the ones hunting for her, but the agents involved in the other four events are all left unspecified, serving to keep the focus of the narrative on Elizabeth Smart. The verbs and impersonalized forms used in the text are listed in table 6.3 along with descriptions of their valence, type, trajector elaboration, and agent identity; those without overt elaboration of the trajector are shown in bold, and agents not made explicit in the text are in italics.

Example 6 gives a glossed transcription of one ASL translation of this text. The translation includes seventeen verbs, listed in table 6.4. In

TABLE 6.3. *Verbs in English Text Prompt: Elizabeth Smart*

Token	Valence	Verb Type	Elaboration of Trajector	Identity of Agent
found	divalent	passive	**not overtly elaborated**	*someone*
hunt	divalent	nominal	earlier in the discourse	police
was reported	divalent	passive	**not overtly elaborated**	*someone*
abducted	divalent	adverbial	**not overtly elaborated**	*someone*
was found	divalent	passive	**not overtly elaborated**	*someone*
was reunited	divalent	passive	**not overtly elaborated**	*someone*
were tipped	divalent	passive	in a by phrase	two callers
had seen	divalent	active	as the subject - relative clause	two callers
knew	divalent	active	as the subject - relative clause	two callers
was wanted	divalent	passive	**not overtly elaborated**	*police*
questioning	divalent	gerund	**not overtly elaborated**	*police*

addition to producing REMOVE (which Participant C uses for *abducted*) and FIND without overtly elaborating their trajectors, she also uses the verb DISTRIBUTE without an explicit agent. Several monovalent verbs without specified agents also appear. Those without overt elaboration of the trajector are shown in bold in the table, and agents not made explicit in the text are in italics.

6. **Gloss of Participant C's translation of the Elizabeth Smart text**

   QUOTE NEWSPAPER ITSELF C-N-N / HAPPEN IN S-L-C / TALK-ABOUT ELIZABETH SMART / GIRL SELF[L1] UMM REMOVE[L1→L2] PAST HAPPEN PAST UMM PAST SUMMER RIGHT PAST SUMMER REMOVE[L1→L2] / PAST ... FIND LIVE PAST WEDNESDAY / BACK[L2→L1] WITH FAMILY GROUP-TOGETHER[L1] FINISH-SET BUT <HOW POLICE FIND-O-U-T HOW>rhq / PRO[→|text|] SAY TWO ... TRUE PRO[→|?|] HAVE PICTURE #OF S-U-S-P-E-C-T PRO[→|?|] / SEEM DISTRIBUTE / TWO PEOPLE SEE[→|picture|] CALL[→|police|] T-I-P CALL[→|police|] INFORM[→|police|] THAT KNOW WHERE LOCATION

The discourse structure of this ASL narrative is very similar to the one about paleontology. The signer opens by producing several utterances

Token	Valence	Verb Type	Elaboration of Trajector	Identity of Agent
HAPPEN	monovalent	plain	not overtly elaborated	*the event*
TALK-ABOUT	monovalent	plain	not overtly elaborated	*the text*
REMOVE	**divalent**	**depicting**	**not overtly elaborated**	*someone*
HAPPEN	monovalent	plain	not overtly elaborated	*the event*
REMOVE	**divalent**	**depicting**	**not overtly elaborated**	*someone*
FIND	**divalent**	**plain**	not overtly elaborated	*someone*
BACK	stative	locative	not overtly elaborated	*someone*
FIND O-U-T	divalent	plain	as the subject	POLICE
SAY	monovalent	plain	as the subject	PRO3 - the text
HAVE	divalent	plain	as the subject	PRO3 - generic reference
SEEM	stative	plain	not overtly elaborated	*n/a*
DISTRIBUTE	**divalent**	**depicting**	**not overtly elaborated**	*someone*
SEE	divalent	indicating	as the subject	TWO PEOPLE
CALL	divalent	indicating	earlier in the discourse	TWO PEOPLE
CALL	divalent	indicating	earlier in the discourse	TWO PEOPLE
INFORM	divalent	indicating	earlier in the discourse	TWO PEOPLE
KNOW	monovalent	plain	earlier in the discourse	TWO PEOPLE

without overtly elaborated trajectors. The first two of these utterances set the scene and describe the topic, and they are followed by several utterances expressing the events in the Elizabeth Smart case. Elizabeth Smart has already been overtly mentioned and is understood as the most focused entity in the discourse at this point, but each of these utterances relates to her as the patient rather than the agent. The agents, though understood by the addressee through context, are unexpressed—completely unspecified and not prominent in the discourse. The next section includes a few agent-focused utterances with overt subjects and then alternates between agent-focused and defocused agent expressions, analogous to what was seen in the English prompt text. The final section of the narrative begins with a fully focused agent expressed overtly as a subject, TWO PEOPLE, followed by several clauses without overt subjects, for which the trajectors are understood to be elaborated at the discourse level by TWO PEOPLE, which is the most prominent discourse entity throughout the section and to the end of the narrative.

Five divalent verbs without explicitly mentioned agents appear in the English text: "reported," "abducted," "found," "reunited," and "wanted." The question of how defocused agents are expressed in the ASL is best answered by examining how the signers express each of these concepts in their translations. The verb "was tipped" is also used passively in the English text, but its agent is made explicit in a *by*-phrase; the ASL translations for it are included in the following discussion. Not all concepts expressed as divalent events in the English text retain that same form in the ASL translations. Each signer's version is slightly different from the others.

The reporting of Elizabeth's abduction, the first of the agentless events in the English text, is included only in Participant D's translation. It is attributed to a specific agent, Elizabeth's parents, and expressed as an active sentence (figure 6.8). The verb TAP$^{\rightarrow y}$ is an indicating verb that is directed toward the entity to be mapped onto its landmark; in this utterance TAP$^{\rightarrow y}$ is used without having established the identity of the surrogate to correlate with its landmark. After producing this clause, the

PARENTS	TAP$^{\rightarrow\vert?\vert}$	(pause)
SEARCH	(pause)	FIND

FIGURE 6.8. *Indicating verb with no overtly elaborated landmark, followed by two verbs with unspecified agents.*

signer blends with the unspecified surrogate understood as the landmark of TAP$^{\rightarrow|?|}$, and produces the verbs SEARCH and FIND. Between each of the verbs, the signer opens her hands to a relaxed position and directs her gaze at the addressee; these brief pauses, combined with the changes in the directionality of her eye gaze, signal shifts in the understood agent for each verb, paralleling the semantic content of the English text.

The three verbs in this utterance exemplify various ways of defocusing an entity using indicating verbs and surrogate blending. The trajector of the first verb, TAP$^{\rightarrow|?|}$, is overtly elaborated by the subject nominal PARENTS, providing an agent-focused construal. For the landmark of TAP$^{\rightarrow|?|}$, however, even though an area of space to conceptually map onto the patient is indicated through directionality of movement, orientation of the fingertips, and eye gaze, the entity that space is intended to refer to is not identified in the current utterance, nor has it been identified previously. In this case, the patient of the utterance is construed with reduced focus because it is unspecified. The next verb takes this same unnamed but indicated location in space and uses it as the surrogate with which the signer blends herself, representing the unspecified agent of SEARCH. The final verb in figure 6.8 is FIND, which occurs with eye gaze toward the addressee, signaling narration rather than representation of an entity. Because FIND is produced with no overt subject elaborating its trajector, the agent doing the finding is defocused.

The next divalent event expressed with a defocused agent in the English text is the abduction; each of the four signers chose a different option for expressing this act. Participant C uses REMOVE with a defocused agent; there is no nominal that elaborates the trajector either in the utterance or anywhere in the previous narrative. Participant A uses GONE as an adjectival predication, keeping Elizabeth Smart in focus as the subject. Participant D also uses an adjectival predication but with MISS instead of GONE.[2] Participant B does not mention the abduction in her translation.

The third defocused agent event in the prompt text is expressed passively as "was found." All four of the signers use the verb FIND in subjectless clauses. Three of them do not have an overtly elaborated trajector; the trajector in the fourth instance, though not overtly elaborated in the same clause, is understood to be elaborated by the most prominent entity

2. MISS is generally used when someone missed an event or opportunity; it is typically not used when discussing objects that are missing, so this sign choice was most likely influenced by the word "missing" in the English text.

in the discourse at that moment: in this case the overt nominal POLICE, which occurs as the subject of the immediately preceding clause.

The next concept expressed passively in the English text is that of the police being tipped as to the suspect's whereabouts. Unlike the other passive forms discussed so far, this one is produced with a *by*-phrase overtly naming the agent ("two callers"). This evokes a construal in which the focus on the agent is reduced through a lack of prominence. The resulting level of agent focus is different from that evoked in passive constructions without *by*-phrases. Passive constructions without *by*-phrases do not express the agent, making it both nonprominent and unspecified and therefore defocused in both ways. In passive constructions that do have *by*-phrases, the agent is specified, but its expression occurs in an oblique, a grammatical position of lesser prominence, which reduces the level of focus on it.

In response to this overt but reduced focus agent in the English text, three of the four participants expressed the agent as an overt subject. TWO PEOPLE and TWO CALLER are used as the overt subjects in these utterances, which evoke an agent-focused rather than a reduced focus or defocused agent construal.

Participant B, however, expresses the event with POLICE as the subject. As figure 6.9 shows, she initially fingerspells the English past participle T-I-P-P-E-D[3] and then follows this with another predication, GET T-I-P FROM SOMEONE. It is unclear whether the signer produced the second predication as further clarification or as a self-correction, but she hesitates slightly between the two predications. Both the fingerspelled participle and the use of GET in this context show considerable direct influence from the English text.

The information that Elizabeth has been reunited with her family is also expressed passively in the English prompt text. Only two signers mention it in their translations; they both do so using the intransitive verb BACK, for which Elizabeth serves as the focused entity, previously overtly expressed and therefore understood through the discourse structure as elaborating the trajector of BACK.

---

3. Fingerspelled past participles are sometimes used to express a meaning analogous to that of an English passive (Cole 2000). Though anecdotally native ASL users often mention fingerspelled verbs as translation equivalents of English passives, in the data analyzed here they are extremely rare (this is the only one in the narrative data). Further research on their frequency and the conditions in which they are used is warranted.

POLICE T-I-P-P-E-D (hesitation)

GET T-I-P FROM SOMEONE

FIGURE 6.9. *An instance of a fingerspelled past participle.*

Finally, for the concept of the suspect being "wanted for questioning," three different strategies were used in the elicited translations. One participant left out the concept entirely. One participant fingerspelled S-U-S-P-E-C-T, including the implication that he was "wanted" within that nominal. The other two signers both produced PRO⁻ᐟ|suspect| WANT following the English word order exactly and shifting their bodies back during the production of the verb to indicate that the trajector of WANT is not the entity indicated by the pronoun. This form is similar to what Janzen, O'Dea, and Shaffer (2001) label as an ASL passive except that it is not viewed from the patient's perspective; the information is presented from the narrator's perspective, not identified with either the agent or the patient. The resulting signed utterance is strongly influenced by English word order, and both participants who used this form seemed to have reactions to it. Participant A starts to sign PERSON after WANT but switches in midsign, signaling a self-correction, and reexpresses the concept with an agent-focused construal: this time the agent, POLICE, is in subject position, and the "wanted person" is the patient, expressed in object position (figure 6.10). Participant D did not self-correct the utterance, but at the end of her translation just a few seconds later, she made a side comment, stating that it felt awkward.

PRO$^{\rightarrow|suspect|}$ WANT   PERS . . .

POLICE   WANT   PRO$^{\rightarrow|suspect|}$

FIGURE 6.10. *False start showing switch from patient focus to agent focus.*

As we have seen, all four translations of the Elizabeth Smart text evoked defocused agent construals, using subjectless clauses without overt elaboration of the trajector either in the clause or earlier in the narrative.

ASL TEXT DATA: REM SLEEP

Scientific writing, especially research description, is a discourse genre that contains a preponderance of passive constructions. Within a single text, most of these passive constructions will imply the same entity as the agent: the researcher (or, more likely, research assistants carrying out work on the researcher's behalf). Because the identity of the agent is relatively fixed over the course of the text and is easily and directly inferred from the content, research description as a discourse type would seem to lend itself more naturally to expression with an agent-focused construal when translated into ASL. If, as some books and curriculum materials suggest (Mikos, Smith, and Lentz 2001; Kelly 2001; Mindess et al. 2006), ASL tends toward direct expression and agent focus, one would expect the data elicited in response to the research-description text to show this construal shift. The English prompt paragraph about a REM sleep experiment was included specifically to test this hypothesis.

TABLE 6.5. *Verbs in English Text Prompt: REM Sleep Experiment*

Token	Classification	Valence	Elaboration of Trajector	Identity of Agent
show	active	divalent	as the subject	experiments
can help	active modal	trivalent	as the subject	REM sleep
learn	active	divalent	as the subject	you - generic
were taught	**passive**	**divalent**	**not overtly elaborated**	*researchers*
were awakened	**passive**	**divalent**	**not overtly elaborated**	*researchers*
entered	active	divalent	as the subject	they - volunteers
were awakened	**passive**	**divalent**	**not overtly elaborated**	*researchers*
got	active	divalent	as the subject - relative clause	people - volunteers
tested	stative	monovalent	as the subject	people - volunteers
performing	gerund	divalent	earlier in the discourse	people - volunteers

The REM sleep experiment prompt text, given in example 7, consists of five sentences and contains nine verbs. Six of these verbs are active and three of them are passive (table 6.5). The paragraph also contains a nominalized impersonal form *performing,* which is derived from a transitive verb.

7. **English Text Prompt: REM Sleep Experiment**

Experiments show that REM sleep definitely can help you learn better. In one test, volunteers **were taught** a new skill. That night, some of them **were awakened** whenever they entered REM sleep. The others **were awakened** the same number of times, but only during non-REM sleep. The next day, the people who got their REM sleep tested better than the others at *performing* the new skill.

The first sentence uses three active clauses and an infinitive clause to set up the experiments as the topic and state the results. The rest of the sentences explain the process used during a REM sleep experiment; they alternate between passive constructions (explaining what the researchers did) and active constructions (explaining the participants' actions).

The paragraph contains three passive constructions. In each of these, the understood agent is the "researcher," but no explicit mention of the person or persons who carried out these actions appears anywhere in the paragraph. None of the passive constructions contain a *by*-phrase. The participants are the patient in all three passive constructions; the nominals naming them occur in subject position. The second clause of the second sentence and both clauses of the final sentence are active constructions that describe the participants' actions.

Semantically, two entities are involved in the events described in the paragraph: the volunteer research subjects and the researchers who are conducting the experiment. Only the volunteers are ever overtly identified.[4] The agent performing the actions involved in conducting the experiment is defocused in the English text by the use of passive constructions and never overtly mentioned. The context is identified in the first sentence as an experiment; the addressee infers the "experimenter" or some "research assistant(s)" as the actor in all of the passive sentences in this context.

As mentioned earlier, it would have been possible to express the implied agent overtly in the ASL translations of this text; examining the data, however, shows clearly that this was not the case. All four participants defocused the agent performing the actions involved in conducting the experiment. The "experimenter" is never overtly mentioned in any of their translations. Just as in the English prompt text, the ASL descriptions focus on the experimental procedures and the experiences of the research participants, leaving the researcher unstated and defocused.

Example 8 gives a glossed transcription of a representative example translation of this text, and table 6.6 lists the verbs used. The valence of each verb is listed along with the verb type, the method used to elaborate the trajector of each verb, and the understood (or explicit) agent in the event encoded by each verb. Agents that are not explicitly mentioned in the text are given in italics. The verbs shown in boldface type encode two-participant events with animate agents that are not overtly expressed.

8. **Gloss of Participant C's translation of the REM sleep experiment text**

EXPERIMENT / R-E-M SLEEP EXPERIMENT / SAY DECIDE SPLIT-TWO-GROUPS

---

4. In all but one of the utterances "the volunteers" are the patient, expressed in the subject position of a passive construction. In the final sentence, the "volunteers" are the subject of the stative verb "tested."

Token	Valence	Verb Type	Elaboration of Trajector	Identity of Agent
SAY	**divalent**	**plain**	**not overtly elaborated**	*the text*
DECIDE	**divalent**	**plain**	**not overtly elaborated**	*researcher*
SPLIT-TWO-GROUPS	monovalent	depicting	not overtly elaborated	*researcher*
TEACH	**divalent**	**plain**	**not overtly elaborated**	*researcher*
TEACH	**divalent**	**indicating**	**not overtly elaborated**	*researcher*
SLEEP	monovalent	plain	as the subject	ONE GROUP
BOTHER+	**divalent**	**indicating**	**not overtly elaborated**	*researcher*
TAP+	**divalent**	**indicating**	**not overtly elaborated**	*researcher*
WAKE-UP+	monovalent	plain	earlier in the discourse	ONE GROUP
BOTHER	**divalent**	**indicating**	**not overtly elaborated**	*researcher*
BOTHER+	**divalent**	**indicating**	**not overtly elaborated**	*researcher*
BOTHER+	**divalent**	**indicating**	**not overtly elaborated**	*researcher*
D-O	monovalent	fingerspelled	earlier in the discourse	ONE GROUP
DO	monovalent	plain	as the subject	ONE GROUP

PRO$^{\rightarrow|groupA|}$ (false start) / TRUE <BOTH>top TEACH NEW SKILL /
TEACH+ DO-EVERYTHING PERFECT / #THEN DIVIDE-TWO-
GROUPS / PRO$^{\rightarrow|groupA|}$ SLEEP OVERNIGHT / BOTHER$^{\rightarrow|groupA|}$
+ TAP$^{\rightarrow|groupA|}$+ WAKE-UP+ DURING R-E-M SLEEP SO-YOU-
HAVE-THAT / HAPPEN <PRO$^{\rightarrow|groupB|}$>top BOTHER$^{\rightarrow|groupB|}$ ONLY
DURING N-O-N-R-E-M SLEEP BOTHER$^{\rightarrow|groupB|}$+ / OVERNIGHT
TRUE-BUSINESS PRO$^{\rightarrow|groupA|}$ UMM <TRUE BOTHER$^{\rightarrow|groupA|}$
+ DURING R-E-M SLEEP>top PRO$^{\rightarrow|groupA|}$ WEAK-PERFORM NOT
D-O W-E-L-L / PRO$^{\rightarrow|groupB|}$ DO BETTER UMM THAT NEW SKILL

All four signers establish the context of an experiment in the first sentence. For example, Participant B uses the utterance shown in figure 6.11.
Once the context of an experiment has been established, it serves as the
conceptual reference point for the rest of the text. The participants continue the narrative, producing nonovert subject clauses for which the addressee understands the "researcher" as the implied, but defocused, agent.

<TOPIC>top   R-E-M   SLEEP   EXPERIMENT

FIGURE 6.11. *Utterance establishing conceptual reference point of the text.*

In the English prompt text, only three verbs attributed actions to the unstated researcher, and each of them is expressed passively from the patient's perspective. Despite the lack of any overt identification of the agent in all of the ASL translations, participants A and C each have nine verbs expressed from the researcher's perspective. Participants B and D each produce four verbs from the researcher's perspective. Since all of these events are expressed from the agent's perspective rather than the patient's, they do not follow the pattern of prototypical passives; the ASL structures use lack of specificity to reduce focus on the agent, but they are not passive.

The vast majority of defocused agent verbs produced in response to this text were indicating verbs, including TAP, BOTHER, and TEST. As shown in figure 6.12.a–c, all four signers employed these indicating verbs in the same manner, using the movement and orientation of the signs to indicate locations to the signers' left and right as conceptually mapped onto the landmarks, identifying the patients in the events. For all of these signs, the initial location is in neutral space close to the signer, a position that is not indicative of any conceptual space to map onto the trajector; therefore, the clauses containing these verbs are subjectless and have no indication of the entity corresponding to their trajector.[5] Their landmarks were elaborated earlier in the narrative through overt identification and mapping to the same spaces, which are here indicated in the phonological form of the verbs.

None of the signers explicitly identified an entity as the agent for these indicating verbs; the ending locations had previously been established as token spaces representing the two groups of research participants. In all of these examples, the actions of the researcher are described—waking up the sleeping participants, interrupting their sleep, and testing them the

5. Similar examples were discussed in chapter 4.

a. directed toward an entity established to the left
(group awakened while in REM sleep)

TAP→|group in REM sleep|

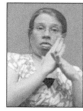

1-BOTHER→|group in REM sleep| 1-TEST→|group in REM sleep|

b. directed from the signer as unspecified agent toward an entity
established to the right (group awakened when not in REM sleep)

TAP→|group not in REM sleep|

BOTHER→|group not in REM sleep| TEST→|group not in REM sleep|

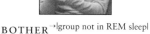

c. directed toward entities established both to the left and to the right
(both groups of participants)

TAP[simultaneous]→|both groups| TAP[alternating]→|both groups|

FIGURE 6.12. *Verbs indicating landmarks only.*

next morning—but no explicit mention of the researcher appears anywhere in any of the ASL narratives.

ASL TEXT DATA: TEQUILA MAKING

Process descriptions are specifically intended to focus on the product being made rather than on any of the agentive entities involved. In English this is primarily accomplished through the use of agentless passive constructions with verbs that semantically encode physical tasks. In ASL, physical tasks are predominantly expressed through the use of surrogate blending, so this prompt text was included to elicit data that would show how surrogate blending interacts with agent defocusing at the narrative level.

There are twenty-one verbs in the English prompt paragraph about how tequila is made, given here as example 9. Sixteen of the verbs are in passive constructions (including two in infinitive form, two in present-perfect constructions, and one following a modal); all sixteen are shown in boldface type in example 9. In addition to passive verbs, the paragraph also contains two constructions with stative verbs, two active constructions, and the infinitive form of the intransitive verb *mature*.

9. English Text Prompt: Tequila
    Tequila **is named** for the town in which it **was** first **produced:** Tequila, province of Talisco, Mexico. It **is produced** from the blue agave plant.
    It takes ten years for the blue agave plant to mature, and only four liters of tequila **can be produced** from each plant. The leaves **are removed,** and the hearts **are taken** to the *tequilers* **to be cooked** and **mashed.**
    The mash **is placed** in tanks for fermenting. The Spaniards introduced the process of this distillation, which separated the alcohol from the fermented mash. The product **was called** *nino mezcal de Tequila.*
    Silver tequila **is bottled** directly at distillation. *Reposado* tequila **is bottled** after it **has been aged** for several months in wooden tanks. Anyejo tequila **is aged** in oak barrels for at least one year before it **is bottled.**
    Tequila is the only alcoholic beverage that identifies a country; it **has been glorified** in movies and songs.

TABLE 6.7. *Verbs in English Text Prompt: Tequila*

Token	Valence	Verb Type	Elaboration of Trajector	Identity of Agent
is named	divalent	passive	not overtly elaborated	*generic*
was produced	divalent	passive	not overtly elaborated	*tequila makers*
is produced	divalent	passive	not overtly elaborated	*tequila makers*
takes	monovalent	stative	as the subject	it - dummy subject
to mature	monovalent	infinitive	earlier in the discourse	the plant
can be produced	divalent	passive	not overtly elaborated	*tequila makers*
are removed	divalent	passive	not overtly elaborated	*tequila makers*
are taken	divalent	passive	not overtly elaborated	*tequila makers*
to be cooked	divalent	infinitive	earlier in the discourse	the Tequilers
(to be) mashed	divalent	infinitive	earlier in the discourse	the Tequilers
is placed	divalent	passive	not overtly elaborated	*tequila makers*
introduced	divalent	active	as the subject	the Spaniards
separated	divalent	active	as the subject - relative clause	the process of this distillation
was called	divalent	passive	earlier in the discourse	the Spaniards
is bottled	divalent	passive	not overtly elaborated	*tequila makers*
is bottled	divalent	passive	not overtly elaborated	*tequila makers*
has been aged	divalent	passive	not overtly elaborated	*tequila makers*
is aged	divalent	passive	not overtly elaborated	*tequila makers*
is bottled	divalent	passive	not overtly elaborated	*tequila makers*
is	monovalent	stative	as the subject	Tequila
has been glorified	divalent	passive	not overtly elaborated	*generic*

Table 6.7 lists the twenty-one verbs, along with their valence and type. The fourth column describes the elaboration of the verb's trajector, and the identity of the agent in the event encoded by each verb is given in the fifth column. Agents not explicitly mentioned in the text are given in italics. Verbs that encode a two-participant event with an animate agent that is not overtly specified are shown in boldface type.

The opening sentence of the text contains two passive clauses: the first clause, "Tequila is named for . . . ," introduces the topic of the text, and the second clause, "in which it was first produced," along with the shift to present tense, "is produced," in the following sentence, provides the theme for the remaining text, namely the production of tequila.

The majority of the verbs in the text refer to an unstated agent understood to be any or all of the people involved in tequila production. These generic "makers of tequila" serve as the agent throughout most of the text. The agent of the initial and final clauses is also unspecified; an addressee would understand it to be "people" broadly conceived and in a generic sense. The remaining verbs in the text are monovalent, with the exception of the verb "separated," which has the impersonalized nominal "distillation" as its subject, and the verb "introduced," which has the only animate agent in an active sentence in the entire text: "the Spaniards."

Participant A's translation of the tequila text is glossed in example 10. Table 6.8 lists the verbs she used. The second column states the valence of each verb, the third column lists the verb type, the fourth column indicates the method used to elaborate the trajector of each verb, and the fifth column gives the identity of the agent in the event encoded by each verb. Any agents not explicitly mentioned in the text are given in italics. The verbs shown in boldface type are those that encode two-participant events with animate agents that are not overtly expressed.

10. **Gloss of Participant A's translation of the tequila text**

 TEQUILA T-E-Q-U-I-L-A / <TRUE TEQUILA NAME FROM WHERE>rhq TOWN FAR-THERE T-E-Q-U-I-L-A THERE / PART #OF T-A-L-I-S-C-O MEXICO index

 <TEQUILA>top <MAKE FROM WHAT>rh BLUE A-G-A-V-E PLANT / <THAT PLANT>top GROW TEN YEAR GROW FINISH / <THAT EACH+ PLANT index>top MAKE+ FOUR LITER #OF TEQUILA

 index REMOVE LEAVES REMOVE / <THAT CENTER PART>top BRING TO MAKE++++++ COOK++ MASH+ COOK++ / <NAME MASH+>rh M-A-S-H / PRO$^{→||left|}$ PUT IN TANK / BOIL SWIRL-

AROUND BECOME ALCOHOL F-E-R-M-E-N-T ALCOHOL
BECOME ALCOHOL

    PRO.poss^{→|right|} SPAIN ONE WHO INF . . . TEACH^{→||left|}+ HOW
MAKE+ D-I-S-T-I-L-L index^{→||left|}

    THAT SEPARATE ALCOHOL FROM COOK++ M-A-S-H
SEPARATE <THAT RESULT index>top <NAME WHAT>rhq
N-I-N-O M-E-Z-C-A-L D-E T-E-Q-U-I-L-A

    SILV . . . HAVE DIFFERENT KIND TEQUILA <SILVER
T-E-Q-U-I-L-A>top PRO^{→||left|} SEPARATE STRAIGHT TO
B-O-T-T-L-E BOTTLE

    R-E-S---R-E-P-O-S-A-D-O T-E-Q-U-I-L-A index^{→|forward|}
LEAVE IN WOOD depict: barrel SEVERAL MONTH++ FINISH
THEN MOVE-OBJECT IN BOTTLE

    A-N-Y-E-J-O T-E-Q-U-I-L-A PRO^{→|forward right|} LEAVE WOOD O-A-K
depict: barrel LEAVE+ ONE-YEAR LEAVE+ THEN MOVE-OBJECT
BOTTLE

In all four the ASL translations, as in the English prompt text, the vast
majority of the verbs do not have overtly elaborated agents. Whereas in
the English text these verbs were expressed in passive constructions, in
the ASL texts they occur in clauses without overt subjects in the types of
syntactic structures described in chapter 4. This is exemplified by the text
glossed in example 10 and shown in table 6.8. In this signer's entire narrative, only three verbs have overt subjects, and two of them refer to the
same entity: the inanimate blue agave PLANT. Just as in the English text,
the only animate agent overtly mentioned is the Spaniards.

The twenty-three verbs for which the trajector is not overtly elaborated
all encode divalent events. All but three of them have the generically
understood "makers" of tequila as the understood agent. Two of the three
with other agents are tokens of CALLED, which has the broadly conceived
notion "people" as its agent, and the third is a token of HAVE used without a subject as an existential.[6]

The structure of the other signers' narratives are similar to that shown
in table 6.8. None of them explicitly name the people involved in the
making of tequila. Two of the other translations contain only one overt
subject each: the Spaniards are the agent in a subject-verb-object construction with a transitive verb in Participant C's translation, and the opening
sentence of Participant D's translation has a subject-verb-prepositional

6. As discussed in chapter 4.

TABLE 6.8. *Verbs Used in ASL Translation of English Process Description Text: Participant A*

Token	Valence	Verb Type	Elaboration of Trajector	Identity of Agent
MAKE	divalent	plain	not overtly elaborated	makers
GROW	monovalent	plain	as the subject	THAT PLANT
GROW	monovalent	plain	earlier in the discourse	THAT PLANT
MAKE	divalent	plain	as the subject	EACH PLANT
REMOVE	divalent	depicting	not overtly elaborated	makers
REMOVE	divalent	surrogate	not overtly elaborated	makers
BRING	divalent	plain (locative)	not overtly elaborated	makers
MAKE++++++	divalent	depicting	not overtly elaborated	makers
COOK++	divalent	depicting	not overtly elaborated	makers
MASH+	divalent	depicting	not overtly elaborated	makers
COOK++	divalent	depicting	not overtly elaborated	makers
CALLED	divalent	indicating	not overtly elaborated	generic
MASH+	divalent	surrogate	not overtly elaborated	makers
PUT	divalent	plain (locative)	not overtly elaborated	makers
BOIL	monovalent	plain	earlier in the discourse	leaves, mash

SWIRL-AROUND	monovalent	depicting	earlier in the discourse	leaves, mash
BECOME	stative	plain	earlier in the discourse	leaves, mash
BECOME	stative	plain	earlier in the discourse	leaves, mash
TEACH	trivalent	indicating	as the subject	SPAIN>TOP ONE
MAKE	divalent	plain	not overtly elaborated	makers
D-I-S-T-I-L-L	divalent	plain	not overtly elaborated	makers
SEPARATE	divalent	plain	not overtly elaborated	makers
COOK++	divalent	depicting	not overtly elaborated	makers
SEPARATE	divalent	plain	not overtly elaborated	makers
CALLED	divalent	indicating	not overtly elaborated	generic
HAVE	divalent	plain	not overtly elaborated	existential
SEPARATE	divalent	surrogate	not overtly elaborated	makers
LEAVE	divalent	indicating	not overtly elaborated	makers
MOVE-OBJECT	divalent	surrogate blend	not overtly elaborated	makers
LEAVE	divalent	indicating	not overtly elaborated	makers
LEAVE+	divalent	indicating	not overtly elaborated	makers
LEAVE+	divalent	indicating	not overtly elaborated	makers
MOVE-OBJECT	divalent	surrogate blend	not overtly elaborated	makers

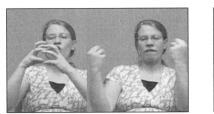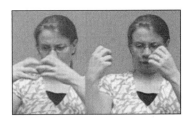

a. dv: REMOVE+   LEAVES   surrogate blend: REMOVE+

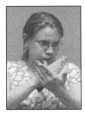

b. dv: COOK++   dv: COOK+   dv: COOK++

FIGURE 6.13. *Depiction of action and surrogate blend with unspecified agent.*

phrase structure, but the referent, "the text," is inanimate. Some of the utterances with defocused agents are nonovert subject clauses with plain verbs, but the predominant way of reducing focus on the agent(s) in these process descriptions is through the use of surrogate blends with unspecified entities and depicting verbs produced without any overt mention of the agent performing the action being depicted.

For example, Participant A uses a verb-object syntactic structure with a depicting verb representing the removal of leaves, followed immediately by a surrogate blend depicting an unspecified agent performing the leaf removal (figure 6.13a). She then expresses the cooking and mashing processes, using depicting verbs inflected for continuous aspect with nonmanuals and multiple repetitions with reduced sign size while gazing directly at the addressee (in this case the camera) (figure 6.13b).[7]

When describing these same processes, the others signers also use depicting verbs and/or surrogate blends without explicitly named agents. Participant D, for example, produces three utterances without explicitly identified agents in this section: a topic-verb structure with an unspecified surrogate blend for the leaf removal (figure 6.14a), the plain verb COOK in a rhetorical question (figure 6.14b), and then an aspectually modified verb depicting MASH (figure 6.14c). Participant C uses aspectually

7. During the final repetition of COOK, which is aspectually marked, her gaze has returned to the English prompt paragraph displayed on the computer screen.

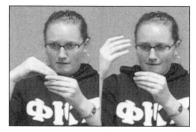

a. surrogate "remove leaves"   b. COOK   c. dv: MASH

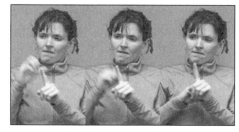

d. dv: "remove leaves"   e. dv: COOK

FIGURE 6.14. *Depicting verbs and surrogate blends without explicitly named agents.*

inflected verbs depicting "removal of leaves" (figure 6.14d) and COOK (figure 6.14e) but keeps her gaze on the addressee rather than producing these signs as surrogate blends.

The tequila text was included to elicit a process description in ASL and to determine how surrogate blending interacts with agent defocusing. The translation data show that surrogate blends were readily used even when the entity with which the signer is understood to be blended has not been previously identified. The resulting highly prominent but unspecified agents are construed with reduced focus relative to those in overt subject utterances. The ASL narratives evoke a construal in which the process and product—rather than the individuals involved—are in focus, analogous to the construal evoked in the English text.

CONCLUSION

In chapter 4 we saw ASL utterance forms that could be used to evoke construals of defocused agents, and in chapter 5 we saw the variety of utterance types that evoke reduced focus agents. The data described here in chapter 6 show that all of these types of utterances also occur in elicited narrative data. The participants use divalent verbs in clauses in which the trajector is not overtly elaborated even when an entity corresponding to that verb's trajector has not previously been established in the narrative. When this occurs, the entity inferred by the addressee as agent is not prominent or specified, and the resulting construal is one in which the agent is defocused.

The translation tasks used in the data collection allowed each individual to make choices about how to express each concept, and the richness of the elicited data reflects that, evidencing a variety of strategies within these subjectless clause constructions utilizing plain verbs, indicating verbs, and surrogate blending. Each utterance affects the prominence and specificity with which the agent is expressed and may result in a change in the level of focus on the agent within the narrative as a whole.

The ASL utterance types used to evoke construals of events without focusing on the agent in the narrative data are parallel to those in the individual sentence data described in chapters 4 and 5 in that they are primarily clauses that do not include overt subjects and for which the identity of the agent is not expressed overtly anywhere in the narrative. In the individual sentence data, the majority of utterances are produced using plain verbs in subjectless clauses; in the ASL narrative data discussed here, signers include indicating verbs and depicting verbs just as readily as plain verbs. Indicating verbs are used without any mention of the entity to be mapped onto the space indicated as corresponding to the agent. Verbs that depict actions also frequently occur without overt elaboration of their trajectors, making the agent performing the action visible but unspecified.

Constructed action through the use of surrogate blends is common in ASL narratives (Metzger 1994; Liddell and Metzger 1998); even while limiting focus on the agent in narratives, signers produce surrogate blends. Rather than explicitly introducing an entity to serve as the surrogate in the blend, when signers want to use a surrogate blend but keep the agent out of focus, they simply blend with a surrogate whose identity has not been overtly established. These blends with unspecified surrogates are especially prevalent in the data collected in response to process descriptions. Through unspecified surrogate blends, signers are able to directly convey actions while keeping the focus of the narrative on the process itself rather than on the agent. Although the agent is visible in these signed surrogate blends, the addressee is not told the agent's identity. The meaning expressed with unspecified surrogate blends is therefore analogous to the semantic content of the corresponding agentless passive sentences.

In stretches of ASL narrative discourse, the prominence and specificity with which an agent is expressed in the clause interacts with the level of focus that has previously been given to that entity in the discourse. If an entity is made prominent in the discourse through overt specification, it can serve to elaborate the trajector of a verb (or multiple verbs) following it in the discourse (Liddell 2003). The relevant finding in the current analysis is that clauses without overt subjects can be used in ASL even when the agent has not been previously established in the discourse and even when the agent's identity is never mentioned. Subjectless forms are used not only with plain verbs but also with indicating verbs and even when the signers produce surrogate blends in which they construct the actions of the unspecified agent. When divalent verbs occur in any of these types of subjectless clauses where the trajector has not already been overtly elaborated, the resulting construal is one in which the focus on the agent is reduced or removed at both the clause and the narrative levels.

Chapter 7

Agent Focus in ASL-to-English Translation

The data from the ASL-to-English sentence and text translation tasks, presented in chapters 4, 5 and 6, show that ASL users do have ways to defocus the agent. They do so by leaving the agent unexpressed, producing utterances in which the trajector is not overtly elaborated and which evoke a construal similar to that expressed by English passive constructions. The third and final task included in the study was to determine whether the reverse was also true: when signers are presented with an ASL text containing clauses without overtly elaborated trajectors, do they understand them to evoke a defocused agent construal? Do they consider the evoked construals to be semantically parallel to those of English passive constructions?

In order to test this, an ASL-to-English text translation task was conducted. The ASL prompt text, glossed in example 1, is a description of the process of making pencils (Stratyi & Taylor, 1998).

1. Glossed Transcript of ASL Text Prompt: How Pencils Are Made
   <PENCIL>top PEOPLE CALL <LEAD>q head-shake SHOULD CALL
   G-R-A-P-H-I-T-E MIX WITH C-L-A-Y / MUST MIX FIRST TOSS-
   IN STRONG MACHINE depict:machine-shape TOSS-IN C-L-A-Y
   TOSS-IN G-R-A-P-H-I-T-E MIX STIR FINISH / THEN TOSS-IN
   depict:extrusion CRANK depict:extrusion MAKE SPAGHETTI
   LOOK-LIKE depict:extrusion / depict:long-thin-cylindrical TOSS-
   IN HOT COOK HARD BAKE COOK QUOTE SOLID / FINISH
   dv:REMOVE-FROM-OVEN DV:CUT-UP P-I-E-C-E-S THAT'S-THAT
   PUT-ASIDE
       <WOOD WHAT>rh <depict:cover PENCIL index>top MUST
   BEST C-E-D-A-R <OTHER>q head-shake <index C-E-D-A-R>
   top SMOOTH NOT depict:splinter <WHY>rh dv:SHARPEN
   depict:splinter head-shake depict:smooth NICE C-E-D-A-R
       #OK SUPPOSE PENCIL depict:cover depict:length++ dv:OPEN-
   COVER depict:thin-straight-object <SPAGHETTI>top dv:PLACE-
   IN-COVERS dv:CLOSE-COVER GLUE dv:SET-COVER-IN-PLACE

depict:full-length-of-cover GLUE FINISH / PAINT FINISH /
dv:CUT-SECTIONS C-U-T / dv:CHOP-OFF-END dv:ATTACH-
TO-END E-R-A-S-E-R / BIG-FINISH-BECOME-SMALL PENCIL
THERE-YOU-HAVE-IT

This text was initially chosen because it was a process description and contained many utterances without overly elaborated trajectors. As a process description, the overall focus of the text is on the steps and actions involved rather than on the people doing the work. In order to achieve this discourse-level focus on the process, the focus needs to be shifted away from the agent(s) at clause level.

The analysis of data from the English-to-ASL tasks had not yet been conducted, so it was not clear what specific ASL agent-defocusing strategies were incorporated in the text. It was known only that the text contained many utterances without overt trajector elaboration and that the overall effect of the text was a non-agent-focused process description. After the analysis of the data from the English-to-ASL tasks had been conducted, the ASL text prompt was analyzed more closely to determine the clausal and discourse-level structures that were used to evoke defocused agent construal. The discussion of the structures and construals within the prompt text are given in the following section.

To complete the task, participants were asked to write an English translation of the ASL video clip. This gave them free choice in how to express the content of the text in English. Their choice of particular English structures can be seen as evidence of the ways that they are construing the situations as evoked by the ASL prompt text.

This chapter describes the elicited English texts produced by the study participants in response to the ASL video clip. This "reverse elicitation" served as a test case of sorts; not only did the participants produce certain forms to express reduced-focus and defocused agent construals in response to the English-to-ASL tasks, but, as addressees, they also construed these forms as evoking defocused agent construals, as evidenced by the use of passive constructions and a variety of other impersonalization strategies in their English translations.

STRUCTURE AND CONSTRUAL IN THE ASL PROMPT TEXT

Analysis of the ASL prompt text shows that its discourse structure parallels that found in the elicited ASL text data. The same variety of syntactic forms are included, using clause-level defocused and reduced focus agents interactively with the discourse structure to create the overall nonagent focus. As table 7.1 shows, only the first three verbs have trajectors that are overtly elaborated in the text. The rest of the verbs all profile relations in which the identity of the agent is unexpressed. The bold rows mark verbs for which the agent is construed as defocused or with reduced focus; the trajectors of those verbs are not overtly elaborated anywhere in the narrative. Their implicit agents (i.e., the understood or assumed identity of trajectors that are not explicitly elaborated) are given in italics.

The structure of this narrative is remarkably parallel to the ASL translations produced by the participants in response to the English text prompts, especially the process description of how tequila is made. The trajector of the first verb in the text is overtly elaborated by the noun PEOPLE, expressed in subject position. This agent-focused utterance is followed by two more clauses that do not contain overt trajector elaboration but for which the trajector is understood to correspond to that in the previous clauses. These utterances serve to establish the overall topic and context for the rest of the text.

Once the context of the text has been established as the process of making pencils, this becomes the reference point for understanding the following utterances. The signer now shifts to producing verbs alone and verb-object structures without overtly elaborated trajectors. These utterances contain both plain verbs and depicting blends, and many of the depictions are produced as constructed action with unspecified surrogates. The unidentified agents are understood to be the "pencil makers" through recourse to the opening sentences as the context. Because the agents performing the actions involved in the process are defocused, the narrative functions as a description of the process itself rather than as a story about people who make pencils.

Midway through the narrative, the signs glossed as THAT'S-THAT and PUT-ASIDE co-occur with strong head nods and blinking as discourse markers signaling a topic shift. The following section is a tangential explanation of the type of wood that is best for pencils. There, the syntactic structures differ significantly from those in the previous section. Of the thirty-five signs describing the initial steps in the process (from MUST to P-I-E-C-E-S), sixteen (46 percent) are verbs; once the signer shifts to the explanation section (from WOOD to the second instance of C-E-D-A-R), she uses only two verbs out of twenty signs (10 percent). The two verbs

TABLE 7.1. *Verbs in ASL Text Prompt: How Pencils Are Made*

Token	Valence	Verb Type	Elaboration of Trajector	Identity of Agent
CALL	divalent	plain	as the subject	PEOPLE
SHOULD	divalent	modal	earlier in the discourse	PEOPLE
CALL	divalent	plain w/modal	earlier in the discourse	PEOPLE
MUST	monovalent	modal	not overtly elaborated	*makers*
MIX	divalent	depicting blend	not overtly elaborated	*makers*
THROW	divalent	depicting verb	not overtly elaborated	*makers*
THROW	divalent	surrogate blend	not overtly elaborated	*makers*
THROW	divalent	surrogate blend	not overtly elaborated	*makers*
MIX	divalent	depicting verb	not overtly elaborated	*makers*
STIR	divalent	depicting verb	not overtly elaborated	*makers*
THROW	divalent	depicting verb	not overtly elaborated	*makers*
CRANK	divalent	surrogate blend	not overtly elaborated	*makers*
MAKE	divalent	plain	not overtly elaborated	*makers*
THROW	divalent	depicting verb	not overtly elaborated	*makers*
COOK	divalent	plain	not overtly elaborated	*makers*
BAKE	divalent	plain	not overtly elaborated	*makers*
COOK	divalent	plain	not overtly elaborated	*makers*
REMOVE-FROM-OVEN	divalent	surrogate blend	not overtly elaborated	*makers*
CUT-INTO-PIECES	divalent	depicting verb	not overtly elaborated	*makers*
MUST	monovalent	modal	not overtly elaborated	*generic*
SHARPEN	divalent	surrogate blend	not overtly elaborated	*anyone*
OPEN-COVER	divalent	surrogate blend	not overtly elaborated	*makers*
PLACE-IN-COVERS	divalent	surrogate blend	not overtly elaborated	*makers*
CLOSE-COVER	divalent	depicting verb	not overtly elaborated	*makers*
SET-COVER-IN-PLACE	divalent	depicting verb	not overtly elaborated	*makers*
PAINT	divalent	depicting verb	not overtly elaborated	*makers*
CUT-SECTIONS	divalent	surrogate blend	not overtly elaborated	*makers*
CHOP-OFF-END	divalent	surrogate blend	not overtly elaborated	*makers*
ATTACH-TO-END	divalent	depicting verb	not overtly elaborated	*makers*

are a modal, MUST, with no accompanying main verb, and a depiction of the act of sharpening a pencil, which is produced as a surrogate blend. Neither of these two verbs have elaborated trajectors, and their agents are understood to be completely generic.

The signer signals the end of the explanation section with a closed pause (Nicodemus 2009) with hands clasped and a full head nod with closed eyes. The section following this second discourse shift returns to a process description with multiple verb only, verb-object, and topic-verb structures, and the final twenty-five signs include eight verbs (32 percent).

ANALYSIS OF ASL-TO-ENGLISH ELICITED TEXT

Participants were asked to translate the text into written English. One representative translation is given in example 2.

2. **English Translation of ASL Process Description: How Pencils Are Made**

People frequently think that pencils **are made** with lead. This is incorrect. They are actually graphite mixed with clay. There is a large machine that mixes up the clay and graphite. These two ingredients **are mixed** thoroughly. The mixture **is** then **pushed** through a screen that results in a thin spaghetti-like appearance that goes inside the pencil as we know it. These sticks of graphite/clay mix **are** then **baked** at high temperatures to harden them. The other part of pencils are the wood coverings. These **are** only **done** with cedar. The reason for this is they are smooth and less likely to splinter. This is especially good when having to sharpen the pencils. Now, these wood sticks **are cut** into half to allow for the graphite/clay sticks **to be placed** in the middle. The wood halves **are glued** back together. Then the pencils **are coated**. They **are** then **cut** into certain lengths. The erasers **are attached** to the ends, and voila, you have your pencil.

This English translation contains twenty-nine verbs and two impersonal forms derived from the transitive verb "mix": the adjective "mixed" and the noun "mix." All thirty-one tokens are listed in table 7.2 and labeled according to their valence, type, and the ways in which their trajectors are elaborated.

TABLE 7.2. *Verbs Used in English Translation of ASL Process Description: Participant B*

Token	Valence	Verb Type	Elaboration of Trajector	Identity of Agent
think	divalent	active	as the subject	people
are made	**divalent**	**passive**	**not overtly elaborated**	*makers*
is	monovalent	stative	as the subject	this
are	monovalent	stative	as the subject	they
mixed	divalent	adjectival	earlier in the discourse	graphite
is	monovalent	stative	not overtly elaborated	*existential*
mixes	divalent	active	as the subject (relative clause)	machine
are mixed	**divalent**	**passive**	**not overtly elaborated**	*makers*
is pushed	**divalent**	**passive**	**not overtly elaborated**	*makers*
results	monovalent	stative	as the subject (relative clause)	(pushed through screen)
goes	monovalent	active	as the subject (relative clause)	(spaghetti-like sticks)
know	divalent	active	as the subject	we (generic)
mix	**divalent**	**nominal**	**not overtly elaborated**	*makers*
are baked	**divalent**	**passive**	**not overtly elaborated**	*makers*
to harden	monovalent	infinitive	earlier in the discourse	sticks
are	monovalent	stative	as the subject	part
are done	**divalent**	**passive**	**not overtly elaborated**	*makers*
is	monovalent	stative	as the subject	reason
are	monovalent	stative	as the subject	they
to splinter	monovalent	infinitive	earlier in the discourse	they
is	monovalent	stative	as the subject	this
having to	**monovalent**	**modal**	**not overtly elaborated**	*anyone*
sharpen	**divalent**	**infinitive**	**not overtly elaborated**	*anyone*
are cut	divalent	passive	not overtly elaborated	*makers*
to allow	divalent	infinitive	earlier in the discourse	(cut in half)
to be placed	**divalent**	**infinitive**	**not overtly elaborated**	*makers*
are glued	**divalent**	**passive**	**not overtly elaborated**	*makers*
are coated	**divalent**	**passive**	**not overtly elaborated**	*makers*
are cut	**divalent**	**passive**	**not overtly elaborated**	*makers*
are attached	**divalent**	**passive**	**not overtly elaborated**	*makers*
have	divalent	active	as the subject	you (generic)

The translation shows that the participant clearly construed the overall text as process focused rather than agent focused. There are ten passive constructions in the text, twice as many instances of passive than any other verb type used. In addition to using passives to defocus the agent, the elicited English text includes several other impersonalization strategies, including infinitives, nominalizations, stative verbs, and the use of generic *you* as the subject, which all serve to reduce agent focus to varying degrees. This points to the range of levels of focus on the implied agent(s) construed by the participant, as well as to her ability to express this range of focus using various strategies in English.

Most important, the understood but never identified agent that runs throughout the ASL text, namely the pencil makers, is never overtly expressed in the English translation. Most of the clauses with the pencil makers as the understood agent are expressed with passive constructions. The only other two instances are expressed using a nominal and an infinitive, both of which reduce the focus on the pencil makers by impersonalizing the process and not profiling the agent.

CROSS-PARTICIPANT COMPARISON OF ELICITED ENGLISH TEXTS

A comparison of the four English translations reveals strong parallels between them that also correlate directly with the ASL narrative. For example, all of the English translations use the subject "people" in an active construction in the opening sentence, although the verbs used in these clauses vary (see example 3). For the utterance glossed as MIX STIR FINISH / THEN, three of the signers used adverbial clauses beginning with "after," but they chose different ways to convey the mixing and stirring without focusing on the agent, as shown in example 4.

3. Opening Sentence of Each of the Four English Translations
   a. Pencil, people call it lead, but really you should call it graphite . . .
   b. According to this lady, people tend to refer the insides of pencils as "lead" but that's not accurate.
   c. People think pencils are made with lead. That isn't true.
   d. People frequently think that pencils are made with lead. This is incorrect.

4. English Translations for MIX STIR FINISH / THEN
   a. After it is mixed . . .
   b. After that mix is complete . . .
   c. After the mixing process ends . . .

Recall that midway through the ASL narrative, the signer makes a clear shift from process description to explanation and uses only two verbs, both without overt elaboration of their trajectors and that allow for only the most generically conceptualized agents. Only one of the English translations of this part of the narrative contains a passive construction—"these are only done with cedar"—which has a semantically "empty" root verb and thus lends itself to an equally generic assumed agent. On the other hand, thirteen of the verbs in this section are stative. These loosely correlate with the depictions of objects in the ASL narrative. For the unspecified surrogate blend used to depict a pencil being sharpened, three participants expressed the impersonal construal with the generic-reference personal pronoun "you," and the fourth expressed it in an adverbial clause with a modal in gerund form and a plural landmark: "when having to sharpen the pencils."

5. English Translations of ASL Explanation of Wood Used in Pencils
   a. The wood that is used for pencils is cedar. This is the best because it is smooth. When you sharpen your pencil it will be smooth because of the cedar wood.
   b. Now, for the main body of the pencil, the same lady says cedar is the best type of wood to use. It's smooth and doesn't tend to splinter, especially when you sharpen the pencils.
   c. Ok, now we'll talk about the wood casing the pencil comes in. Cedar is the best type of wood for pencils because when you put them in a pencil sharpener, they won't splinter or flake like other wood.
   d. The other part of pencils are the wood coverings. These are only done with cedar. The reason for this is they are smooth and less likely to splinter. This is especially good when having to sharpen the pencils.

Table 7.3 provides a list of the verbs and other impersonal forms used by each participant. Two common patterns emerge: all of the participants used more passive constructions than other verb forms, and all of the participants used a wide variety of English impersonalization strategies.

TABLE 7.3. *Forms Used in Elicited ASL-to-English Process-Description Texts*

Type	A	B	C	D	Total
Passive	7	10	13	11	41
Stative	4	5	2	7	18
Active	4	4	5	3	16
Generic personal pronoun	7	2	2	2	13
Infinitive	1	5	0	3	9
Nominalization	0	2	2	1	5
Existential	0	0	2	1	3
Other	1	1	0	1	3
Indefinite pronoun	0	0	0	0	0
Total	24	29	26	29	108

Thus, in response to an ASL narrative with trajectors that are predominantly not overtly elaborated, none of the translations included more than five active sentences with fully specified agents. More than 85 percent of the English clauses were impersonalized, and 38 percent were instances of the passive construction. Taken all together, the participants used passive clauses more than twice as often as any of the other forms. Participant A used generic personal pronouns with the same frequency as passives, but none of the participants used any other verb type more often than passives. In fact, Participant C used as many passive clauses as all the other clause types combined; interestingly, she also used the greatest number of active clauses of any of the four participants.

CONCLUSION

The four participants each produced a variety of impersonal forms in their English translations, which shows that they construe the ASL subjectless utterances without elaborated trajectors as defocused agent expressions similar in semantic content to English passives, while also having a range of reduced-focus options similar to the variety found in the English impersonal system. Passive utterances make up the majority of the verb types used in the elicited texts as a whole. The use of predominantly passive constructions to defocus the pencil makers, interspersed with other impersonalization strategies that reduce focus on agents throughout the text, results in English texts with construals that parallel the construal evoked by the ASL prompt text.

Chapter 8

Conclusion

Appropriate use of the English passive construction can be difficult for deaf English language learners to master (Goldberg and Astley 1986) and is also quite difficult, in my personal experience, to teach effectively. In English language classrooms with deaf students, the teachers often find themselves in the position of explaining the meaning of particular constructions through ASL translations of example sentences, and, without a thorough understanding of how ASL expresses an analogous construal, teachers do not have the necessary foundation to be able to effectively provide such translations. The analysis described in this book seeks to fill that gap by taking the meaning of passive constructions, a defocused agent construal, as the starting point and determining the forms that native signers use to evoke such a construal.

The most common strategy that native signers used to produce translations of English passive sentences was to simply leave the agent unexpressed. Though claims have been made that ASL is more direct than English (see discussion in Hoza 2007) and that ASL uses active voice where English uses passive voice (e.g., Kelly 2001), ASL native signers who were asked to translate English passive sentences only added overt subjects and changed them into "active" sentences in very few cases. Although there may be a certain ASL construction that is syntactically passive, as previous research on agreement verbs suggests (most notably Janzen, O'Dea, and Shaffer 2001), this construction was not the primary way native ASL signers defocused agents in the data analyzed here. Although anecdotal evidence and preliminary research (Cole 2000) also suggest that fingerspelling the past participle employed in English passives (such as K-I-L-L-E-D) is an ASL strategy for defocusing the agent, this was also not the predominant technique used in the elicited data. Participants did not struggle with the translation tasks they were given, and they expressed very little discomfort about being asked to produce agent-defocused construals. All four signers, in all of the translation tasks, readily produced utterances that simply did not overtly mention the agent, thereby evoking the defocused agent construal through both prominence and specificity.

The relative level of focus on an entity in a linguistic utterance is determined by the prominence and specificity with which that entity is expressed. Prominence is assigned to entities based on grammatical role; for example, subjects are more prominent than objects, which are in turn more prominent than obliques (Croft 1990). Specificity can be adjusted through the use of nominal structures that vary in the extent of semantic content they evoke. Consider, for example, the relative specificity of the generic plural pronoun "they" and a full nominal like "teachers," which is in turn less specific than a singular nominal such as "the researcher" or an even more specific name of an individual.

In English the primary strategy for defocusing the agent is the agentless passive construction. The phonological structure of such constructions consists of a subject, a form of *to be,* and the past participle of a transitive root verb. The past participle encodes a semantic structure in which the focal prominence is shifted away from the agent. The root verb's landmark becomes the trajector, giving focal prominence to the patient, which is expressed in subject position. The agentless passive construction does not contain a *by*-phrase, so the agentive participant is unspecified because there is no nominal identifying it. The agent is defocused in terms of both level of prominence (lack of trajector status) and level of specification (not overtly expressed).

When asked to translate English passive sentences into ASL, native ASL users predominantly produced utterances without overt subjects, retaining the defocused agent construal, albeit through a different form. The verbs used in ASL defocused agent utterances do not differ from those used in agent focused constructions, so there is no change in trajector, as occurs in the English passive construction. The ASL verbs are divalent and therefore profile both a trajector and a landmark, but the trajector is not overtly elaborated, resulting in a phonological form without a subject. With no nominal identifying the agent, the trajector is unspecified. Because there is a single verb form for both agent-focused and agent-defocused utterances, however, no shift of primary focal prominence to another element takes place. The lack of specificity of the agent results in a construal in which the agent is defocused, but the retained profiling of both the trajector and the landmark makes these utterances distinct from passives.

In an ASL utterance, the ultimate level of focus on the agent varies with the extent of information the verb provides about that entity. In ASL, verbs can be categorized with respect to the amount of information they provide about the involved participants: plain verbs do not identify their participants within their phonological form; indicating verbs reference the location of a conceived entity in the signing space; and utterances containing surrogate blends represent participants visually as the signer constructs their actions.

Plain verbs, indicating verbs referencing a mental space mapping for the agent referent, and surrogate blends depicting agentive action can be used in clauses without overt nominals elaborating their trajectors. When plain verbs that encode relations between an agent and a patient are used without mentioning the agent's identity, the result is a construal in which the agent is defocused. Indicating verbs that encode spatial reference to their trajectors give some prominence to the agent even when its identity is not overtly specified, resulting in a construal with reduced agent focus. Similarly, depiction of the action of a surrogate encodes the agent in a visually prominent form that can be produced without specifying the surrogate agent's identity; the resulting interaction between high prominence and low specificity results in a construal with reduced focus on the agent. It may be argued that whereas English passive tokens without *by*-phrases "completely" defocus their agents, ASL subjectless clauses with verbs that indicate agents or include surrogate blends do incorporate aspects of the agent in a visually salient way. They can therefore be considered to retain a slight focus on the agent relative to ASL subjectless clauses with plain verbs, although the agent's identity is still entirely implicit since no separate nominal naming it exists in the utterance (or anywhere in the previous discourse).

In addition to utterances without overt lexical elaboration of the trajector, the data also contain a few utterances in which the trajector is elaborated but either in a position of reduced prominence (e.g., the given answer to a rhetorical question) or by the use of an underspecified lexical form, such as a pronoun. When these forms are used, the resulting construal is one in which the agent is reduced in focus. These structures exist but are not prevalent in the elicited data; it is possible that their structure was the result of influence from the English prompt sentences; thus the readiness of their use in naturalistic settings remains questionable.

The conclusion that ASL utilizes a range of forms that express construals with differing levels of focus is not problematic in light of the fact that similar variety in the impersonal forms of English and other spoken languages has been shown to exist (Shibatani 1985; Marín-Arrese

2008).[1] Impersonalized forms in English range from nominalizations, existentials, and passive constructions, which fall at the agent-defocused end of the spectrum, to active sentences with fully specified nominal subjects at the agent-focused end.

The ASL utterances with the least focus on the agent are those with both reduced prominence and a lack of specificity; these constructions are semantically equivalent to, though syntactically distinct from, the English passive construction. Plain verbs without overt subjects fall at the defocused agent end of the spectrum of ASL utterances, which range in their level of agent focus. Hence, nonovert subject utterances with plain verbs used when agents are not overtly expressed are most semantically parallel to an English passive construction without a *by*-phrase. Indicating and depicting verbs without overt subjects and surrogate blends defocus their agents, but not quite to the same extent. Without explicit mention of the event participant being incorporated into the blend, the agent is unspecified but not completely removed from the utterance. Thus, subjectless utterances with indicating verbs and those incorporating agentive surrogate blends do not defocus their agents to the same extent as plain verbs with unspecified agents, but their agents are less in focus than overtly elaborated trajectors, even those with indefinite or generic reference pronouns.

In ASL, utterances that do not include overt elaboration of the trajector encode construals that parallel those encoded in the range of English impersonal forms, in which prominence and specificity interact to produce reduced agent focus. Just as English uses a number of impersonal forms to defocus the agent to various extents (Shibatani 1985; Marín-Arrese 2008), so ASL also has a variety of impersonalization strategies to express agents and to vary the degree of focus on them.

IMPLICATIONS AND DIRECTIONS FOR FUTURE RESEARCH

As discussed earlier, the main impetus for conducting this research was to provide foundational linguistic research to aid English teachers working with deaf students. Through the course of the research, the implications for ASL teachers and for ASL/English interpreters also became abundantly clear.

For deaf students learning English it is important to understand the construal evoked by the English passive in order to be able to use it

---

1. As discussed in chapter 2.

effectively, and understanding the linguistic parallels in ASL can help them to do so. The utterance types found in the elicited data can be used by teachers to develop "translations" of example passive sentences in English. More important, further research should explore the ways that this understanding supports student learning and development of writing skills, leading to more effective pedagogical approaches. Collaborative work involving linguists and teachers can continue the research goals initiated here and ideally lead to positive outcomes for deaf students.

One of the main findings of this research is that clauses without overt subjects, previously known to be used when the agent is already prominent in the discourse (Liddell 2003), can also be readily produced in discourse contexts in which the agent has not previously been identified. Prior to the current study, ASL was understood to allow clauses without overt elaboration of the trajector only when the trajector's identity had been overtly elaborated earlier in the discourse. Curriculum materials for ASL courses (Mikos, Smith, and Lentz 2001) reflect this understanding, teaching students to set up the characters first and then describe or show their actions. Example ASL narratives often use this structure, establishing the narrative participants early on and then expressing the events that occurred without overtly renaming the participants.

Based on the data presented here, advanced ASL students should be introduced to the concept of agent focus and taught that they can adjust the level of focus on a given entity in ASL in a variety of ways. Rather than being limited to always introducing the participants at the outset, advanced ASL users should be comfortable with making linguistic choices to reduce the focus on an agent in the appropriate discourse contexts.

Finally, ASL/English interpreters, as advanced users working with both English and ASL, should be familiar with the range of agent focus present in both languages. When presented with an English utterance that defocuses the agent, interpreters should have the underlying knowledge necessary to consider the implications of that construal and make choices in their ASL production that would allow for the appropriate analogous construal. Conversely, when presented with an ASL utterance in which the agent is not overtly mentioned, the range of options available for defocusing the agent in English should be part of the interpreter's repertoire.

The implications are wide ranging for users of ASL and English, and much remains to be done to expand upon the current study. In addition to the utterances elicited in response to translation tasks, further research should include the elicitation of defocused agent construals using nonlinguistic prompts such as videos or pictures to reduce the possible impact of English on the ASL expressions. Conversational and narrative ASL data could also be analyzed for the relative focus on agents in a variety of utterances to determine when and where defocused agent utterances are used in naturally occurring discourse. Applied research using the current data and findings to develop potential classroom materials would be beneficial to teachers of both ASL and English. Analysis of interpretations of defocused agent utterances both from English into ASL and from ASL into English would expand our understanding of the impact of interpreters' linguistic choices related to the level of agent focus.

References

Baker-Shenk, C., and D. Cokely. 1980. *American Sign Language: A Teacher's Resource Text on Grammar and Culture*. Silver Spring, MD: T. J. Publishers.

Chen Pichler, D., and J. A. Hochgesang. 2009. An Overview of Possessives and Existentials in American Sign Language. In *Possessive and Existential Constructions in Sign Languages*, ed. P. Perniss and U. Zeshan, 213–33. Sign Language Typology Series no. 2. Nijmegen: Ishara.

Cole, D. 2000. Course paper. Department of Linguistics and Interpretation, Gallaudet University. Cited in *Grammar, Gesture, and Meaning in American Sign Language*, ed. S. K. Liddell, 369. Cambridge: Cambridge University Press, 2003.

Croft, W. 1990. *Typology and Universals*. Cambridge: Cambridge University Press.

———. 1998. The Structure of Events and the Structure of Language. In *The New Psychology of Language: Cognitive and Functional Approaches to Language Structure*, vol. 1, ed. M. Tomasello, 67–91. Mahwah, NJ: Erlbaum.

———. 2005. Logical and Typological Arguments for Radical Construction Grammar. In *Construction Grammars: Cognitive Grounding and Theoretical Extensions*, ed. J.-O. Östman, 273–314. Philadelphia: Benjamins.

Dudis, P. 2002. Grounded Blends as a Discourse Strategy. In *Turn Taking, Fingerspelling, and Contact in Signed Languages*, ed. C. Lucas, 53–72. Washington, DC: Gallaudet University Press.

———. 2004. Body Partitioning and Real-Space Blends. *Cognitive Linguistics* 15(2): 223–38.

Emmorey, K. 1994. The Confluence of Language and Space in Sign Language. In *Language and Space*, ed. P. Bloom. Cambridge, MA: MIT Press.

Goldberg, A. E. 1995. *Constructions: A Construction Grammar Approach to Argument Structure*. Chicago: University of Chicago Press.

———. 1998. Patterns of Experience in Patterns of Language. In *The New Psychology of Language: Cognitive and Functional Approaches to Language Structure*, ed. M. Tomasello, 203–19. Mahwah, NJ: Erlbaum.

———. 2005. Argument Realization. In *Construction Grammars: Cognitive Grounding and Theoretical Extensions*, ed. J.-O. Östman, 17–43. Philadelphia: Benjamins.

———. 2006. *Constructions at Work: The Nature of Generalizations in Language*. Oxford: Oxford University Press.

Goldberg, J. P., and R. H. Astley. 1986. *Revising Your Writing: A Handbook of Solutions to Common Grammar and Usage Problems for Hearing-Impaired Students*. Lexington, MA: Ginn.

Hoza, J. 2007. *It's Not What You Sign, It's How You Sign It: Politeness in American Sign Language*. Washington, DC: Gallaudet University Press.

Isenhath, J. O. 1990. *The Linguistics of American Sign Language*. Jefferson, NC: McFarland.

Janzen, T., B. O'Dea, and B. Shaffer. 2001. The Construal of Events: Passives in American Sign Language. *Sign Language Studies* 1(3): 281–310.

Jespersen, O. 1924. *The Philosophy of Grammar*. London: Allen and Unwin.

Kegl, J. A. 1990. Predicate Argument Structure and Verb Class Organization in the ASL Lexicon. In *Sign Language Research: Theoretical Issues*, ed. C. Lucas, 149–75. Washington, DC: Gallaudet University Press.

Kelly, J. E. 2001. *Transliteration: Show Me the English*. Alexandria, VA: RID Press.

Kemmer, S. 1993. *The Middle Voice*. Amsterdam: Benjamins.

Kitagawa, C., and A. Lehrer. 1990. Impersonal Uses of Personal Pronouns. *Journal of Pragmatics* 14(5): 739–59.

Klima, E. S., and U. Bellugi. 1979. *The Signs of Language*. Cambridge, MA: Harvard University Press.

Lane, H., R. Hoffmeister, and B. Bahan. 1996. *A Journey into the Deaf-World*. San Diego: DawnSignPress.

Langacker, R. W. 1987. *Foundations of Cognitive Grammar*, vol. 1. Stanford, CA: Stanford University Press.

———. 1988. The Nature of Grammatical Valence. In *Topics in Cognitive Linguistics*, ed. B. Rudzka-Ostyn, 91–125. Amsterdam: Benjamins.

———. 1991. *Foundations of Cognitive Grammar*, vol. 2. Stanford, CA: Stanford University Press.

———. 2000. *Grammar and Conceptualization*. Berlin: de Gruyter.

———. 2001. Cognitive Linguistics, Language Pedagogy, and the English Present Tense. In *Applied Cognitive Linguistics II: Language Pedagogy*, ed. M. Pütz, S. Niemeier, and R. Dirven, 3–39. Berlin: de Gruyter.

———. 2002. *Concept, Image, and Symbol: The Cognitive Basis of Grammar*, 2nd ed. Berlin: de Gruyter.

———. 2006. Dimensions of Defocusing. In *Voice and Grammatical Relations: In Honor of Masayoshi Shibatani*, ed. T. Tsumoda and T. Kageyama, 115–37. Philadelphia: Benjamins.

———. 2008. *Cognitive Grammar: A Basic Introduction*. New York: Oxford University Press.

Liddell, S. K. 1980. *American Sign Language Syntax*. The Hague: Mouton.

———. 1995. Real, Surrogate, and Token Space: Grammatical Consequences in ASL. In *Language, Gesture, and Space*, ed. K. Emmorey and J. Reilly, 19–41. Hillsdale, NJ: Erlbaum.

———. 2000. Indicating Verbs and Pronouns: Pointing Away from Agreement. In *The Signs of Language Revisited: An Anthology to Honor Ursula Bellugi and Edward Klima*, ed. H. Lane and K. Emmorey, 303–20. Mahwah, NJ: LEA.

———. 2003. *Grammar, Gesture, and Meaning in American Sign Language*. Cambridge: Cambridge University Press.

Liddell, S. K. and M. Metzger. 1998. Gesture in Sign Language Discourse. *Journal of Pragmatics,* 30:657–97.

Lieven, E., and M. Tomasello. 2008. Children's First Language Acquisition from a Usage-Based Perspective. In *Handbook of Cognitive Linguistics and Second Language Acquisition,* ed. P. Robinson and N. Ellis, 168–96. New York: Routledge.

Loew, R. 1983. Roles and Reference in American Sign Language: A Developmental Perspective. PhD diss., University of Minnesota.

Lucas, C., R. Bayley, and C. Valli. 2001. *Sociolinguistic Variation in American Sign Language*. Washington DC: Gallaudet University Press.

Marín-Arrese, J. I. 2008. Construal and the Use of Impersonalization Strategies in English and Spanish in an FLL Context. In *Proceedings of the 33rd International LAUD Symposium: Cognitive Approaches to Second/Foreign Language Processing: Theory and Pedagogy,* 430–63. Essen: LAUD.

Metzger, M. 1994. Constructed Dialogue and Constructed Action in American Sign Language. In *Sociolinguistics in Deaf Communities,* ed. C. Lucas. Washington, DC: Gallaudet University Press.

Mikos, K., C. Smith, and E. M. Lentz. 2001. *Signing Naturally, Level 3*. San Diego: DawnSignPress.

Mindess, A., with T. K. Holcomb, D. Langholtz, and P. Moyers. 2006. *Reading between the Signs: Intercultural Communication for Sign Language Interpreters*. Boston: Intercultural Press.

Morgan, G. 1999. Event Packaging in British Sign Language Discourse. In *Storytelling and Conversation: Discourse in Deaf Communities,* ed. E. A. Winston, 27–58. Washington, DC: Gallaudet University Press.

Nicodemus, B. 2009. *Prosodic Markers and Utterance Boundaries in American Sign Language Interpretation*. Washington, DC: Gallaudet University Press.

Padden, C. 1988. *Interaction of Morphology and Syntax in American Sign Language*. New York: Garland.

———, and T. Humphries. 1988. *Deaf in America: Voices from a Culture*. Cambridge, MA: Harvard University Press.

———. 2005. *Inside Deaf Culture*. Cambridge, MA: Harvard University Press.

Shibatani, M. 1985. Passives and Related Constructions: A Prototype Analysis. *Language* 61(4): 821–48.

Stokoe, W. C. 1960. *Sign Language Structure*. Studies in Linguistics Occasional Papers 8. Buffalo: University of Buffalo Press.

———, D. Casterline, and C. Croneberg. 1965. *A Dictionary of American Sign Language on Linguistic Principles*. Washington, DC: Gallaudet College Press.

Stratiy, A. P., and M. M. Taylor. 1998. *Pursuit of ASL: Interesting Facts Using Classifiers*. Edmonton, Canada: Interpreting Consolidated.

Svartvik, J. 1966. *On Voice in the English Verb.* The Hague: Mouton.

Talmy, L. 2000. *Toward a Cognitive Semantics.* Vol. 2, *Typology and Process in Concept Structuring.* Cambridge, MA: MIT Press.

———. 2003. Concept Structuring Systems in Language. In *New Psychology of Language.* Vol. 2, *Cognitive and Functional Approaches to Language Structure,* ed. M. Tomasello, 15–46. Mahwah, NJ: Erlbaum.

Taylor, J. R. 2002. *Cognitive Grammar.* Oxford: Oxford University Press.

Tomasello, M., ed. 2003. *New Psychology of Language: Cognitive and Functional Approaches to Language Structure,* vol. 2. Mahwah, NJ: Erlbaum.

Van Cleve, J. V., and B. A. Crouch. 1989. *A Place of Their Own: Creating the Deaf Community in America.* Washington, DC: Gallaudet University Press.

Van Hoek, K. 1997. *Anaphora and Conceptual Structure.* Chicago: University of Chicago Press.

Verhagen, A. 2007. Construal and Perspectivization. In *The Oxford Handbook of Cognitive Linguistics,* ed. D. Geeraerts and H. Cuyckens, 48–81. Oxford: Oxford University Press.

Wilbur, R. B. 1987. *American Sign Language: Linguistic and Applied Dimensions.* Boston: Little, Brown.

———. 1994. Foregrounding Structures in American Sign Language. *Journal of Pragmatics* 22(6): 647–72.

Wolfart, H. C. 1991. Passives with and without Agents. In *Linguistic Studies Presented to John L. Finlay,* ed. H. C. Wolfart, 171–90. Winnipeg: Algonquian and Iroquoian Linguistics.

Index

Figures and tables are indicated by f and t following the page number.

by-phrases (*continued*)
 prominence reduction via word
  order, 11, 73

clause structures, 10
Cognitive Grammar (CG), 9, 10, 14,
 37
conceptual blending. *See also* surrogate
 blends
 defocused agents and, 28–29, 28–
  29f, 65–68, 66–67f
 unspecified surrogates in, 65–68,
  66–67f
conditional topic-verb structure, 60
"The Construal of Events: Passives
  in American Sign Language"
  (Janzen, O'Dea, & Shaffer), 31
construals. *See also* defocused agents
 active vs. passive voice, 11–12, 19
 agent-focused, 5
 defined, 1–2
 form and meaning linked in, 2
contextual understanding of agents,
 96–97
correspondences, 11

declarative clauses, 51
defocused agents
 in ASL, 22–24, 35–76
 in ASL-to-English translations,
  110–19, 113t, 115t, 118t
 conceptual blending and, 28–29,
  28–29f, 65–68, 66–67f
 in English-to-ASL sentence translations, 37–40, 39t
 fingerspelling of past participle, 92,
  120
 future research directions, 123–25
 impersonalization strategies for,
  21–22
 indicating verbs and, 25–26, 30–31,
  57–65, 59–65f
 with nonovert subjects, 26–28,
  43–54, 43–44f, 47–48f, 52–53f
 with overt subjects, 40–42, 41t, 42f
 in passive voice, 12, 120

prominence and, 19–21, 20t, 73–
 76, 74–75f
range of agent defocused in ASL,
 121–23
relevant features, 25–34
specificity and, 19–21, 20t
surrogate blends and, 29–30, 107
underspecification of subjects, 68–
 73, 69–73f
depicting predication, 37, 108
depicting verbs, 38
discourse
 conceptual blending in, 28–29
 defocused agents in, 77–109
 passive voice function of, 11–12, 33
discourse markers, 38, 75–76
divalent verbs. *See also* multivalent
 verbs
 defocused agents and, 121
 in discourse text elicitations, 85, 91,
  108, 109
 impersonalization and, 22
 nonovert subjects and, 26
 passive voice and, 15
 in sentence translations, 36, 37
 topic-verb structure and, 47

ELAN video annotation software, 37
"Elizabeth Smart" text data, 87–94,
 88–89t, 90f, 93–94f
English language, passive voice in,
 15–19, 15–18f, 121
English-to-ASL discourse translations,
 77–109
 "Elizabeth Smart" text data, 87–94,
  88–89t, 90f, 93–94f
 paleontology text data, 78–87, 79t,
  82t, 83–86f
 by-phrases in, 90, 92
 REM sleep text data, 94–100,
  96–97t, 98–99f
 tequila making text data, 100–107,
  102t, 104–5t, 106–7f
English-to-ASL sentence translations,
 25–76
 analysis of, 37–40, 39t

conceptual blending and, 28–29, 28–29*f*, 65–68, 66–67*f*
English-to-ASL sentence translation analysis, 37–40, 39*t*
indicating verbs and, 25–26, 30–31, 57–65, 59–65*f*
with nonovert subjects, 26–28, 43–54, 43–44*f*, 47–48*f*, 52–53*f*
with overt subjects, 40–42, 41*t*, 42*f*
by-phrases in, 23, 37, 122
prominence and, 73–76, 74–75*f*
relevant features, 25–34
surrogate blends and, 29–30
underspecification of subjects, 68–73, 69–73*f*
existentials, 21, 22, 123

fingerspelling, 58–61, 74, 92, 120
focus, concept of, 12–15. *See also* defocused agents

generic-reference pronouns, 21
grammar
form and meaning linked within, 10
meaning of, 2
nonovert subjects, 25
prominence indicated by grammatical position, 40
grammar-construal correspondences, 11

impersonalization strategies
in ASL-to-English translations, 5, 114, 117
defocused agents and, 21–22, 123
in discourse text elicitations, 87
in English-to-ASL sentence translations, 40, 56, 76
language understanding and, 9
nonovert subjects and, 44–45
underspecification of subjects and, 68
implicit agents, 112
indefinite pronouns, 21, 68
indexed locations, 60
indicating verbs
defocused agents and, 25–26, 30–31, 56, 57–65, 59–65*f*, 122

in discourse text elicitations, 91, 108
in English-to-ASL sentence translations, 38
passive voice and, 32
unspecified referents of, 57–65, 59–65*f*
infinitive verbs, 22, 95

Janzen, T., 31, 32, 63, 64, 93

landmarks
in ASL-to-English translations, 117
defined, 14
in discourse text elicitations, 91, 98
divalent verbs and, 121
elaboration of, 62
nonovert subjects and, 26, 45
overt subjects and, 42
topic-verb structure and, 47, 49, 50
unspecified referents with, 60, 64
verb-object structure and, 53
Langacker, Ronald, 2, 9, 15, 17, 37, 45
Language Archiving Portal, 37
language learning and understanding
form and meaning in, 3–4, 35
foundational concepts, 9–11
future research directions, 123–25
passive voice and, 4–5
Liddell, S. K., 27, 29, 30, 37, 58

Marín-Arrese, J. I., 21, 22
Max Planck Institute, 37
monovalent verbs, 37, 88, 101
multivalent verbs
agent focus and, 13, 14
nonovert subjects and, 43
with overt subjects, 40
passive voice and, 15
unspecified referents with, 59

nominalizations, 21, 36, 60, 123
nonovert subjects
in ASL-to-English translations, 118
defocused agents with, 25, 26–28, 43–54, 43–44*f*, 47–48*f*, 52–53*f*
in discourse text elicitations, 84–85, 97, 101, 102, 106

in English-to-ASL sentence translation, 40
nonovert subjects and, 45–46
surrogate blends and, 67
verb-object structure and, 50
stative verbs, 100, 117
Stokoe, William, 3
subjectless clauses, 44, 46, 94, 108, 109
subjects. *See also* nonovert subjects; overt subjects
prominence of, 19
underspecification of, 68–73, 69–73*f*
surrogate blends. *See also* conceptual blending
in ASL-to-English translations, 117
defocused agents and, 29–30, 56, 122
in discourse text elicitations, 91, 100, 106, 107, 108
unspecified, 65–68, 66–67*f*

tequila making text data, 100–107, 102*t*, 104–5*t*, 106–7*f*
topicalization, 27, 37, 47, 49
topic-subject-verb structure, 68
topic-verb structure
in discourse text elicitations, 106
nonovert arguments, 46–50, 47–48*f*
prominence reduction via word order, 75
surrogate blends and, 67
unspecified referents with, 60
trajectors. *See also* defocused agents
in ASL-to-English translations, 111, 118
defined, 14
divalent verbs and, 121
elaboration of, 38, 40, 56, 68, 80, 110
nonovert subjects and, 26, 43, 45, 54
overt subjects and, 42
in passive constructions, 17
prominence reduction via word order, 74

topic-verb structure and, 50
underspecification of subjects and, 73
unspecified referents with, 60, 63, 64, 65
transitive verbs, 95, 114
trivalent verbs, 37. *See also* multivalent verbs

unmarked noun phrases, 38
unspecified referents, 31, 57–65, 59–65*f*

valence properties, 38
verb-object structure, 50–54, 52–53*f*, 106
verbs
affect verbs, 37
agreement verbs, 30, 63, 120
in ASL-to-English translations, 114
"backward verbs," 58
depicting verbs, 38
in discourse text elicitations, 81, 86, 87, 100
divalent. *See* divalent verbs
indicating. *See* indicating verbs
infinitive verbs, 22, 95
monovalent, 37, 88, 101
multivalent. *See* multivalent verbs
in passive constructions, 15–18
plain, 38, 106, 108, 122
stative, 100, 117
topic-subject-verb structure, 68
topic-verb structure. *See* topic-verb structure
transitive, 95, 114
trivalent, 37
verb-object structure, 50–54, 52–53*f*, 106
zero valence, 37
voice. *See* active voice; passive voice

zero valence verbs, 37